The Times of Our Lives

ALSO BY LOUISE L. HAY

BOOKS/KITS
Colors & Numbers
Empowering Women
A Garden of Thoughts:
    My Affirmation Journal
Gratitude: A Way of Life (Louise & Friends)
Heal Your Body
Heal Your Body A–Z
Heart Thoughts
I Can Do It® (book-with-CD)
Inner Wisdom
Letters to Louise
Life! Reflections on Your Journey
Love Your Body
Love Yourself, Heal Your Life Workbook
Meditations to Heal Your Life
    (also in a gift edition)
The Power Is Within You
Power Thoughts
The Present Moment
You Can Heal Your Life
    (also in a gift edition)
You Can Heal Your Life Affirmation Kit
You Can Heal Your Life Companion Book

**COLORING BOOKS/AUDIOCASSETTES
FOR CHILDREN**
The Adventures of Lulu
Lulu and the Ant: A Message of Love
Lulu and the Dark: Conquering Fears
Lulu and Willy the Duck:
    Learning Mirror Work

CD PROGRAMS
Anger Releasing
Cancer
Change and Transition
Dissolving Barriers
Feeling Fine Affirmations
Forgiveness/Loving the Inner Child
Heal Your Body (audio book)
How to Love Yourself
Life! Reflections on Your Journey
    (audio book)
Loving Yourself
Meditations for Personal Healing
Meditations to Heal Your Life (audio book)
Morning and Evening Meditations
101 Power Thoughts
Overcoming Fears
The Power Is Within You (audio book)
The Power of Your Spoken Word
Receiving Prosperity
Self-Esteem Affirmations (subliminal)
Self Healing
Stress-Free Affirmations (subliminal)

Totality of Possibilities
What I Believe/Deep Relaxation
You Can Heal Your Life (audio book)
You Can Heal Your Life Study Course
Your Thoughts Create Your Life

VIDEOCASSETTE
Dissolving Barriers

CARD DECKS
Healthy Body Cards
I CAN DO IT® Cards (a 60-card deck)
I CAN DO IT® Cards for *Creativity,*
    Forgiveness, Health, Job Success, Wealth,
    Self-Esteem, Romance, and *Stress-Free Life*
    (each deck has 12 cards)
Power Thought Cards
Power Thoughts for Teens
Power Thought Sticky Cards
Wisdom Cards

CALENDAR
I Can Do It® Calendar
    (for each individual year)

and

THE LOUISE L. HAY BOOK COLLECTION
    (comprising the gift versions of
    *Meditations to Heal Your Life, You Can
    Heal Your Life,* and *You Can Heal Your Life
    Companion Book*

All of the above are available at your local
bookstore, or may be ordered by visiting:

Hay House USA: **www.hayhouse.com**®
Hay House Australia: **www.hayhouse.com.au**
Hay House UK: **www.hayhouse.co.uk**
Hay House South Africa: **orders@psdprom.co.za**
Hay House India: **www.hayhouseindia.co.in**

Louise's Websites: **www.LouiseHay.com**®
and **www.LouiseLHay.com**®

The Times of Our Lives

Extraordinary True Stories of Synchronicity, Destiny, Meaning, and Purpose

LOUISE L. HAY & FRIENDS

Compiled & Edited by Jill Kramer

HAY HOUSE, INC.
Carlsbad, California
London • Sydney • Johannesburg
Vancouver • Hong Kong • New Delhi

Published and distributed in the United States by: Hay House, Inc.: www.hayhouse.com •
Published and distributed in Australia by: Hay House Australia Pty. Ltd.: www.hayhouse.com.
au • **Published and distributed in the United Kingdom by:** Hay House UK, Ltd.: www.hayhouse.
co.uk • **Published and distributed in the Republic of South Africa by:** Hay House SA (Pty), Ltd.:
orders@psdprom.co.za • **Distributed in Canada by:** Raincoast: www.raincoast.com • **Published
in India by:** Hay House Publications (India) Pvt. Ltd.: www.hayhouseindia.co.in

Editorial supervision: Jill Kramer • *Design:* Tricia Breidenthal

Library of Congress Cataloging-in-Publication Data

The Times of Our Lives : extraordinary true stories of synchronicity, destiny, meaning, and
purpose / Louise L. Hay & friends ; compiled & edited by Jill Kramer.
     p. cm.
  ISBN-13: 978-1-4019-1150-8 (tradepaper) 1. Coincidence--Psychic aspects. 2. Fate and
fatalism. 3. Meaning (Psychology). I. Hay, Louise L. II. Kramer, Jill.
  BF1175.T56 2006
  130--dc22   2006012870

ISBN: 978-1-4019-1150-8

10 09 08 07   4 3 2 1
1st edition, January 2007

Printed in the United States of America

*To all of the contributors who shared
their accounts for this book . . .
and to all of the readers whose lives
will be touched by these stories.*

CONTENTS

Introduction by **Louise L. Hay** ix
  • *My Story* x

THE TIMES OF OUR LIVES

(listed alphabetically by author's surname)

Crystal Andrus: *Love Will Conquer All* 2

Colette Baron-Reid: *Surrender* 10

Frank H. Boehm, M.D.: *No Video Camera Needed* 18

Joan Z. Borysenko, Ph.D.: *Mistakes Are Made in Love's Service* 22

Gregg Braden: *My Friend Merlin* 28

Jim Brickman: *I Love Vanilla!* 34

Sylvia Browne: *My Heaven Is Right Here* 38

Peter Calhoun: *Little Dove* 48

Sonia Choquette: *A Spell of Good Luck* 52

Dr. John F. Demartini: *They Can't Take Away Your Love and Wisdom* . . .60

Dr. Wayne W. Dyer: *The Miracle of the Butterfly* 66

John Edward: *A Spiritual Mail Carrier* 70

Lesley Garner: *Being Human* 78

Keith D. Harrell: *Whatever It Takes to Succeed* 84

Esther and Jerry Hicks: *She Speaks with Spirits!* 94

John Holland: *Heaven's Little Dancer* 106

Immaculée Ilibagiza: *Forgiving the Living* 112

Loretta LaRoche: *You Never Know* 118

Mike Lingenfelter: My Angel, Dakota 124

Denise Linn: Good-bye, Father 132

Monique Marvez: God Made Me Funny and Smart! 138

Dr. Eric Pearl: A Life-After-Death Experience 144

Candace B. Pert, Ph.D.: When You Feel, You Heal 156

John Randolph Price: Our Baby Is Back! 162

Carol Ritberger, Ph.D.: A Different Set of Eyes 168

Ron Roth, Ph.D.: And I Forgive <u>You!</u> 176

Gordon Smith: A Few Slips of the Tongue 180

Ben Stein: The House My Father Built 184

Caroline Sutherland: Breaking Through and Seeing Beyond 188

Alberto Villoldo: The Joy of Living 198

Doreen Virtue, Ph.D.: Reconnecting with My Twin Flame 202

Wyatt Webb: A Sense of Connection 216

Hank Wesselman, Ph.D.: The Caretaker of My Garden 220

Stuart Wilde: Here a Penny, There a Penny 232

Carnie Wilson: It Was about Love 236

Eve A. Wood, M.D.: The Rebirth of a Dream 248

Afterword by **Louise L. Hay**
  • *Playing This Game of Life* 252

About the Editor 254

Editor's note: Some of the excerpted accounts within this
book have been edited from their original versions for space and clarity.

Louise L. Hay

Louise L. Hay is a metaphysical lecturer and teacher and the best-selling author of numerous books, including *You Can Heal Your Life* and *I Can Do It*®. Her works have been translated into 29 different languages in 35 countries throughout the world. For more than 25 years, Louise has assisted millions of people in discovering and using the full potential of their own creative powers for personal growth and self-healing. Louise is the founder and chairman of Hay House, Inc., which disseminates books, audios, and videos that contribute to the healing of the planet.

Websites: **www.LouiseHay.com**® and **www.LouiseLHay.com**®

INTRODUCTION

"Over the years, as I've read the words of the authors who've con-
tributed to this book, I've often thought, <u>What an incredible collection of</u>
<u>ideas, revelations, and inspiration!</u> *I've long wanted to present some of*
the outstanding stories within these works in one place so that you, the
reader, can be as entertained, enlightened, and enthralled as I've been.

"So, within these pages, you'll find some of the most fascinating true
accounts you'll ever come across. The contributors are from virtually every
walk of life and have gone through a diverse array of experiences that
will evoke wonder, awe, laughter, tears, amazement . . . yes, all of these
emotions and more!

"Please enjoy this book, and hopefully it will inspire you to be more
cognizant of the touching, wondrous, and miraculous occurrences that
are a part of your own life.

"But first, I'd like to start out by sharing something very personal
with you. . . ."

— Louise

MY STORY

"Will you tell me a little about your childhood, briefly." This is a request I've posed to so many people who have sought my help. It's not that I need to hear all the details, but I want to get a general pattern of where they're coming from. If they have problems now, the patterns that created them began a long time ago.

When I was a little girl of 18 months, I experienced my parents divorcing. I don't remember that as being so bad. What I do remember with horror is when my mother went to work as a live-in domestic and boarded me out. The story goes that I cried nonstop for three weeks. The people taking care of me couldn't handle that, and my mother was forced to take me back and make other arrangements. How she managed as a single parent inspires my admiration today. Then, however, all I knew and cared about was that I wasn't getting all the loving attention I once had.

I've never been able to determine if my mother loved my stepfather or whether she just married him in order to provide a home for us. But it was not a good move. This man had been brought up in Europe in a heavy Germanic home with much brutality, and he'd never learned any other way to manage a family. My mother became pregnant with my sister, and then the 1930s Depression descended upon us, and we found ourselves stuck in a home filled with violence. I was five years old.

To add to the scenario, it was just about this time that a neighbor, an old wino, as I remember it, raped me. The doctor's examination is still vivid in my mind, as was the court case in which I was the star witness. The man was sentenced to 15 years in prison. I was told repeatedly, "It was your fault," so I spent many years fearing that when he was released he'd come and get me for being so terrible as to put him in jail.

Most of my childhood was spent enduring both physical and sexual abuse, with a lot of hard labor thrown in. My self-esteem got lower and lower, and few things seemed to go right for me. I began to express this pattern in the outside world.

There was an incident in the fourth grade that was so typical of what my life was like. We were having a party at school one day, and there were several cakes to share. Most of the children in this school except for me were from comfortable middle-class families. I was poorly dressed, with a funny bowl haircut, high-topped black shoes, and I smelled from the raw garlic I had to eat every day to "keep the worms away." We never had cake; we couldn't afford it. There was an old neighbor woman who gave me ten cents every week, and a dollar on my birthday and at Christmas. The ten cents went into the family budget, and the dollar bought my underwear for the year at the dime store.

So, on this day we were having a party at school, and there was so much cake that, as they were cutting it, some of the kids who could have had cake almost every day were getting two or three pieces. When the teacher finally got around to me (and of course I was last), there was no cake left. Not one piece.

I see clearly now that it was my "already confirmed belief" that I was worthless and did not *deserve* anything that put me at the end of the line with no cake. It was *my* pattern. *They* were only being a mirror for my beliefs.

When I was 15, I couldn't take the sexual abuse any longer, so I ran away from home and school. The job I found as a waitress in a diner seemed so much easier than the heavy yard work I had to do at my house.

Being starved for love and affection and possessing virtually no self-worth, I willingly gave my body to whoever was kind to me; and just after my 16th birthday, I gave birth to a baby girl. I felt that it was impossible to keep her; however, I was able to find her a good, loving home—I found a childless couple who longed for a baby. I lived in their home for the last four months of my pregnancy, and when I went to the hospital, I had the child in their name.

Under such circumstances, I never experienced the joys of motherhood . . . just the loss, guilt, and shame. I only remember my baby's big toes, which were unusual, like mine. If we ever meet, I'll know for sure if I see her toes. I left when the child was five days old.

I immediately went back home and said to my mother who had continued to be a victim, "Come on, you don't have to take this any longer. I'm getting you out of here." She came with me, leaving my ten-year-old sister, who had always been Daddy's darling, to stay with her father.

After helping my mother get a job as a domestic in a small hotel and settling her into an apartment where she was free and comfortable, I felt that my obligations were over. I left for Chicago with a girlfriend to stay a month—and didn't return for more than 30 years.

In those early days, the violence I experienced as a child, combined with the sense of worthlessness I developed along the way, attracted men into my life who mistreated me and often beat me. I could have spent the rest of my life berating men, and I probably would still be having the same experiences. Gradually, however, through positive work experiences, my self-esteem grew, and those kind of men began to leave my life. They no longer fit my old pattern of unconsciously believing I deserved abuse. I do not condone their behavior, but if it were not "my pattern," they wouldn't have been attracted to me. Now, a man who abuses women does not even know I exist. Our patterns no longer attract.

After a few years in Chicago doing rather menial work, I went to New York and was fortunate enough to become a high-fashion model. Yet, even modeling for the big designers didn't help my self-esteem very much. It only gave me more ways to find fault with myself. I refused to recognize my own beauty.

I was in the fashion industry for many years; and I met and married a fine, educated English gentleman. We traveled the world, met royalty, and even had dinner at the White House. Although I was a model and had a wonderful husband, my self-esteem still remained low until years later when I began the inner work.

One day after 14 years of marriage—just when I was beginning to believe that good things could last—my husband announced his desire to marry another. Yes, I was crushed, but time passes, and I lived on. I could feel things changing, and a numerologist one spring confirmed it by telling me that in the fall, a small event would occur that would change my life.

It was so small that I didn't notice it until several months later. Quite by chance, I'd gone to a meeting at the United Church of Religious Science in New York City. While their message was new to me, something within me said, "Pay attention," and so I did. I not only went to the Sunday services, but I began to take their weekly classes. I was losing interest in the world of beauty and fashion. How many years could I remain concerned with my waist measurement or the shape of my eyebrows? From a high-school dropout who never studied anything, I now became a voracious student, devouring everything I could lay my hands on that pertained to metaphysics and healing.

The Religious Science church became a new home for me. Even though most of my life was going on as usual, this new course of study began to take up more and more of my time. The next thing I knew, it was three years later, and I was eligible to apply to become one of the church's licensed practitioners. I passed the test, and that's where I began, as a church counselor, many years ago.

It was a small beginning. During this time I became a Transcendental Meditator. My church was not giving the Ministerial Training Program for another year, so I decided to do something special for myself. I went to college for six months—at MIU, Maharishi International University—in Fairfield, Iowa.

It was the perfect place for me at that time. During freshman year, every Monday morning we began a new subject, things I had only heard of, such as biology, chemistry, and even the theory of relativity. Every Saturday morning there was a test. Sunday was free, and Monday morning we began anew.

There were none of the distractions so typical of my life in New York City. After dinner we all went to our rooms to study. I was the oldest kid on campus and loved every moment of it. No smoking, drinking, or drugs were allowed, and we meditated four times a day. The day I left, I thought I would collapse from the cigarette smoke in the airport.

Back to New York I went to resume my life. Soon I began taking the Ministerial Training Program. I became very active in the church and its social activities. I began speaking at their noon meetings and seeing clients. This quickly blossomed into a full-time career. Out of the work I was doing, I was inspired to put together the little book *Heal Your Body,* which began as a simple list of metaphysical causations for physical illnesses in the body. I began to lecture and travel and hold small classes.

Then one day I was diagnosed with cancer.

With my background of being raped at five and having been a battered child, it was no wonder I manifested cancer in the vaginal area.

Like anyone else who's just been told they have cancer, I went into total panic. Yet because of all my work with clients, I knew that mental healing worked, and here I was being given a chance to prove it to myself. After all, I'd written the book on mental patterns, and I knew that cancer was a dis-ease of deep resentment that has been held for a long time until it literally eats away at the body. I had been refusing to be willing to dissolve all the anger and resentment at "them" over my childhood. There was no time to waste; I had a lot of work to do.

The word *incurable,* which is so frightening to so many people, means to me that this particular condition cannot be cured by any outer means and that we must go within to find a cure. If I had an operation to get rid of the cancer and didn't clear the mental pattern that created it, then the doctors would just keep cutting Louise until there was no more Louise to cut. I didn't like that idea.

If I had the operation to remove the cancerous growth and also cleared the mental pattern that was causing the cancer, then it wouldn't return. If cancer or any other illness returns, I don't believe that it's because they didn't "get it all out," but rather that the patient has made no mental change. He or she just re-creates the same illness, perhaps in a different part of the body.

I also believed that if I could clear the mental pattern that created this cancer, then I wouldn't even need the operation. So I bargained for time, and the doctors grudgingly gave me three months when I said I didn't have the money.

I immediately took responsibility for my own healing. I read and investigated everything I could find on alternative ways to assist my healing process.

I went to several health-food stores and bought every book they had on the subject of cancer. I went to the library and did more reading. I checked out foot reflexology and colon therapy and thought they would both be beneficial to me. I seemed to be led to exactly the right people. After reading about foot reflexology, I wanted to find a practitioner. I attended a lecture, and while

I usually sat in the front row, this night I was compelled to sit in the back. Within a minute, a man came and sat beside me—and guess what? He was a foot reflexologist who made house calls. He came to my home three times a week for two months and was a great help.

I knew I also had to love myself a great deal more than I had been. There had been little love expressed in my childhood, and no one had made it okay for me to feel good about myself. I had adopted "their" attitudes of continually picking on and criticizing me, which had become second nature.

I'd come to the realization through my work with the church that it was okay and even essential for me to love and approve of myself. Yet I kept putting it off—much like the diet you'll always start tomorrow. But I could no longer postpone it. At first it was very difficult for me to do things like stand in front of a mirror and say things like, "Louise, I love you. I really love you." However, as I persisted, I found that several situations came up in my life where in the past I would have berated myself, and now, because of the mirror exercise and other work, I wasn't doing so. I was making some progress.

I knew I had to clear the patterns of resentment that I'd been holding since childhood. It was imperative for me to let go of the blame.

Yes, I'd had a very difficult childhood with a lot of abuse—mental, physical, and sexual. But that was many years ago, and it was no excuse for the way I was treating myself now. I was literally eating my body with cancerous growth because I hadn't forgiven. It was time for me to go beyond the incidents themselves and to begin to *understand* what types of experiences could have created people who would treat a child that way.

With the help of a good therapist, I expressed all the old, bottled-up anger by beating pillows and howling with rage. This made me feel cleaner. Then I began to piece together the scraps of stories my parents had told me about their own childhoods. I started to see a larger picture of their lives. With my growing understanding, and from an adult viewpoint, I began to feel compassion for their pain, and the blame slowly began to dissolve.

In addition, I hunted for a good nutritionist to help me cleanse and detoxify my body from all the junky foods I'd eaten over the years. I learned that junky foods accumulate and create a toxic body. Junky thoughts accumulate and create toxic conditions in the mind. I was given a very strict diet with lots of green vegetables and not much else. I even had colonics three times a week for the first month.

I did not have an operation; however, as a result of all the thorough mental and physical cleansing, six months after my diagnosis I was able to get the medical profession to agree with what I already knew—*that I no longer had even a trace of cancer!* Now I was able to affirm from personal experience that *dis-ease can be healed if we are willing to change the way we think, believe, and act!*

Sometimes what seems to be a tragedy turns out to become the greatest good in our lives. I learned so much from that experience, and I came to value life in a new way. I began to look at what was really important to me, and I made a decision to finally leave the treeless city of New York and its extreme weather. Some of my clients insisted that they'd "die" if I left them, but I assured them that I'd be back twice a year to check on their progress . . . and, of course, telephones can reach anywhere.

So I closed my business and took a leisurely train trip to California, deciding to use Los Angeles as a starting point. Even though I'd been born there many years before, I knew almost no one anymore except for my mother and sister, who both now lived on the outskirts of the city, about an hour away. We had never been a close family nor an open one, but still, I was quite concerned when I learned that my mother had been blind for a few years, and no one had even bothered to tell me. My sister was too "busy" to see me, so I let her be and began to set up my new life.

My little book *Heal Your Body* opened many doors for me. I began to go to every New Age–type meeting I could find. I would introduce myself, and when appropriate, give out a copy of the little book. For the first six months, I went to the beach a lot, knowing that when I got really busy, there would be less time for such leisurely pursuits. Slowly, the clients appeared. I was asked to speak here and there, and things began to come together as Los Angeles welcomed me. Within a couple of years, I was able to move into a lovely home.

My new lifestyle in Los Angeles was a large leap in consciousness from my early upbringing. Things were going smoothly, indeed. How swiftly our lives can change completely!

One night I received a phone call from my sister, the first communication in two years. She told me that our mother, now 90 and almost deaf, had fallen and broken her back. In one moment, my mother went from being a strong, independent woman to being a helpless child in pain.

She broke her back and also broke open the wall of secrecy around my sister. Finally, we were all beginning to communicate. I discovered that my sister also had a severe back problem that impaired her sitting and walking and which was very painful. She suffered in silence, and although she looked anorexic, her husband didn't know she was ill.

After spending a month in the hospital, my mother was ready to go home. But in no way could she take care of herself, so she came to live with me.

Although I trusted in the process of life, I didn't know how I could handle it all, so I said to God, "Okay, I'll take care of her, but you have to give me help, and you have to provide the money!"

It was quite an adjustment for both of us. She arrived on a Saturday, and the following Friday I had to go to San Francisco for four days. I couldn't leave my mother alone, but I had to go. I said, "God, you handle this. I have to find the right person to help us before I leave."

On the following Thursday, the perfect person had "appeared," and moved in to organize my home for my mother and me. It was another confirmation of one of my basic beliefs: "Whatever I need to know is revealed to me, and whatever I need comes to me in Divine right order."

I realized that it was lesson time for me once again. Here was an opportunity to clean up a lot of that garbage from childhood.

My mother hadn't been able to protect me when I was a child; however, I could and would take care of her now. Between my mother and my sister, a new whole adventure began.

To give my sister the help she asked for presented another challenge. I learned that when I'd rescued my mother so many years ago, my stepfather had then turned his rage and pain against her, and it was my sister's turn to be brutalized. I realized that what started out to be a physical problem was then greatly exaggerated by fear and tension, plus the belief that no one could help her. So here I was, not wanting to be a rescuer and yet wanting to give my sister an opportunity to choose wellness at this point in her life.

Slowly the unraveling began, and it continued until the end of her life. We progressed step by step as I provided an atmosphere of safety while we explored various avenues of healing.

My mother, on the other hand, responded very well. She exercised as best she could four times a day, and her body got stronger and more flexible. I took her to get a hearing aid, and she became more interested in life. In spite of her Christian Science beliefs, I persuaded her to have a cataract removed from one eye. What a joy for her to begin to see again and for us to view the world through her eyes. She was so pleased to be able to read again.

My mother and I found the time to sit and talk to each other in ways we had never been able to before, and a new understanding developed between us. We both became freer as we cried and laughed and hugged together. Of course sometimes she pushed my buttons, but that only told me that there was something further for me to clear.

It is now 2007, and I am 80 years old. My mother left the planet peacefully a number of years ago. I miss her and love her. We completed all we could together, and now we are both free.

(From *You Can Heal Your Life*, Hay House, 1984, 2004)

THE
TIMES
OF OUR
LIVES

⁓

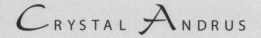

Korby Banner

Crystal Andrus, the author of *Simply . . . Woman!* and *Transcendent Beauty*, is a passionate and powerful speaker, writer, and advocate for women's empowerment. Her message is fortified by a committed spirituality and an inherent desire to help women transcend their limits and soar on the wings of their soul.

One of North America's most dynamic health and fitness experts and nutritionists, she is certified by the American College of Sports Medicine and the Canadian School of Natural Nutrition, and is working toward her Ph.D. in naturopathic medicine. Her dedication to empowering and strengthening the spirit of women can be felt in everything she does—from her weekly radio show, to her successful private coaching practice, to her lectures and workshops, to her active participation on her Website's message forum: **www.crystalandrus.com**.

LOVE WILL
CONQUER ALL

"I was scheduled to give a talk for my alma mater's alumni banquet, and when I first arrived, a beautiful blonde instantly approached me. She had an effervescent smile, and she illuminated the entire room. There was just something about her, and I knew that we were meant to talk again. Within minutes, we were exchanging e-mail addresses.

"Toward the end of my speech—during which I spoke about our relationship with our parents and how our emotions play themselves out through our bodies—I noticed this woman intently listening. Her arms were gently wrapped around her body, and tears were streaming down her face. I intuitively knew that she had a powerful tale to tell. And boy, oh boy, did she ever! It was a story that I knew needed to be shared, so here it is in her own words."

— Crystal

SHERE'S STORY

On April 22, 1953, I came into the world feetfirst, kicking and screaming, about a month early. They say that I was deformed and bruised at birth and certainly nothing much to look at. They called me Shirley (after Shirley Temple), but when I left home at 15, I changed my name to Shere.

3

I don't remember much of my childhood—in fact, it's almost a blank until age 13. Most of what I know about myself has come from stories told to me by neighbors and family members. I do remember my parents saying that I was "ugly, stupid, and a slut." I remember being beaten repeatedly. I remember believing that I was such a horrible creature that I deserved to be beaten. Of course my parents were also struggling—financially and with each other.

From ages 13 to 15, I kept running away. Not far . . . but away from the house. When I was 15, the school stepped in and had me taken out and put into a foster home. I remember leaving with a suitcase of clothes—no toys or books or keepsakes. There were no tears or good-bye hugs . . . I just moved out and barely saw my family (two sisters and a brother) until 1971, when I married my first husband at age 18.

He enjoyed drinking and hitting . . . and I found myself running away once more, looking for any kind of love—in all the wrong places. Within two years, my husband and I were separated; and I again found myself out on the street with my clothes, a few dishes, and some ratty pieces of furniture.

From ages 20 to 25, I went from man to man looking for love and security. I didn't find it. But I *did* find more abusive and controlling men. Only now, as I look back, do I realize how desperate I must have been.

I met my second husband in 1976. He was ten years older, and an extremely generous man. With his two small children, ages four and nine, I was finally going to have the love and family I never had. My new husband adored me and wanted to take care of me, so we moved away to start fresh.

Since I didn't have children of my own—and I wasn't sure if I ever wanted them (afraid of my own "damaged blood")—I found being a stepmom very difficult. I resented my husband's kids and any attention they received from him. Eventually, I found myself feeling insecure again, so I began the search for someone else's "undivided attention." It was the '80s, and the nightclubs were filled with promise. . . . My marriage ended soon after.

Then I met Jeff. He was 10 years younger and 50 years wiser than I was. We dated off and on for seven years, and he was so patient and devoted. I had a hard time committing myself totally to him—and then one day he said that he'd had enough of me and was gone. It was at that moment that I became an adult. It was only then that I realized what I'd lost. Up until that point, I truly thought that I was having so much fun making up for all the lost years that I didn't see it coming.

Months went by, and the pain never went away. My love for Jeff grew stronger, and eventually we found our way back to each other and have never looked back. We've been married 15 years, and our love is one that people write books about.

Somewhere in all this, my ego had begun to run rampant. At age 15, I weighed 200 pounds, thanks to my first job working in a bakery. I found comfort in that warm, loving bread. For my first wedding, I lost the weight, but following the first divorce, I gained it all back and then some—I weighed 220 pounds. My second husband, being the loving and encouraging "father" that he was, introduced me to the game of squash and enrolled me in classes to help me build my self-confidence. I lost the weight and gained plenty of confidence. Well . . . at least it sort of felt like confidence.

I joined a talent agency and did modeling in print work and commercials, and I finally got a regular gig as a TV host. I was totally focused on being so beautiful that no man could resist me—not even the delivery guy. I believed that I was the ugly duckling who had turned into the beautiful swan . . . and I could write a book about all the men I seduced over the years.

Then in 1997, I received a rude awakening when I lost my job. Jeff and I had just purchased a large home, and we had no idea how we were going to pay for it. That same year my father died, and as sad as it was, his death opened up a treasure trove of suppressed emotions. All the "should haves" and "could haves," along with all the fights and the pain, came flooding back in waves. My mother had already died in 1986, and I thought that I'd put that part of my life behind me—but I hadn't.

I was suddenly out of work and feeling so afraid and lost. Waking up every day with no place to go brought forth feelings of failure and reawakened the buried pain of being "stupid." For about a year I moped about in our brand-new, much-too-large house and felt sorry for myself. My health wasn't great, and I was seeing a chiropractor two to three times a week for pain, PMS, and headaches. My visits to the doctor were also frequent, as I complained of stomach pain, constipation, and myriad problems relating to digestion, only to find out that I had irritable bowel syndrome (IBS), as well as an ulcer, a hiatal hernia, *and* endometriosis!

My chiropractor and I became close—after all, I saw more of him than anyone else. One day he presented the idea that I should start thinking about what was causing all my health challenges and think more about prevention—that I should take control of my wellness.

At first I didn't take him seriously because I thought that I knew better. But he eventually got through to me, and I started taking some natural supplements to help balance and build my hormones. Within four months, I was completely free from the ailments of PMS (pain, depression, anxiety, and bloating), which was major for me. This was also the turning point when I started to think outside the box, making my own decisions and taking charge of my life.

For three years, I lived and breathed the "wellness in body, mind, and spirit" philosophy. I attended every lecture, read all the books, subscribed to the health magazines, started working in a health-food store, and began looking into glycobiology and glyconutrients. I was guided to learn meditation and practice yoga; and I sought out new healing modalities—iridology, Reiki, acupuncture, and music therapy. I saw medical doctors who were open to holistic therapies and experienced all the new tests: saliva, inner terrain, blood, you name it—I tried it all. I figured that since I was happily married, I'd now have to settle for being just the "health goddess."

And then in 2000, my soul woke me up.

A mammogram, x-ray, and dreaded biopsy revealed that I had cancer in my right breast. How could this be happening to someone who'd just spent the last three years doing everything she could to get well, stay well, and prevent any sickness?

The next few months were terrifying. The first surgeon I went to had absolutely no sympathy for me, and his bedside manner left a lot to be desired. I went to see his partner in the same office, and their dispositions were like night and day. He was a young man of Asian descent, with an open mind to alternative therapies. His message, however, was the same: I'd have to undergo surgery followed by chemotherapy and possibly radiation. The difference was that he explained the procedure and the possible side effects, and he encouraged me to continue taking alternative therapies if my belief was that strong.

I concluded that the operation and side effects were worse than the disease itself, and even if the disease was removed from my body, the chances of it coming back were high because I hadn't yet determined or faced the reasons why I had been given the gift of cancer in my breast in the first place. So until I knew the reasons, why put my body through the trauma?

My wellness focus changed. Although I had to take care of myself physically—I stopped drinking coffee, soda, and alcohol completely; I ate organic whenever available; I didn't use a dishwasher or microwave; I stopped wearing perfume or toxic nail polish; and I decided to choose a very holistic lifestyle, including natural makeup and cleaning products, purified water, lots of supplements and greens, and an intense regimen of glyconutrients—my focus was now on understanding why the cancer had manifested in my breast.

This took me on a journey that surprised even me. One day during a walk, I spotted a beautiful, soft, grassy area, and I sat down and closed my eyes. I suddenly saw myself surrounded by shimmering bookcases, filled with volumes as far up and out as my eyes could see. I could read the names of the books, and I could touch them and pull them off the shelves. The library was harmonious with nature, and there were gardens and trees mingled throughout. I saw my precious cats who had passed on, and they were happily chasing birds and butterflies through the lush green forest.

I continued to walk into the vastness of this library, and I came across a woman. I barely recognized her at first, and then I realized that it was my mother. She hugged me and said, "Hello, dear. We've been thinking about you," and in that instant, my father appeared. They both looked radiant and translucent. My dad told me that he missed me, and his love for me was never ending . . .

and I immediately understood the depth of his love. I began to cry as I implicitly realized why, in his life as my father, he'd abused me and driven me away. I knew that he truly loved me and that we'd both agreed to reincarnate as father and daughter in this lifetime to learn the lessons that our souls both desperately needed in order to evolve.

In that instant, I forgave myself and them. I felt more love than ever before, and I was sobbing uncontrollably. They both hugged me and said that it was time for me to leave the library and return home. Before they left, I asked them what book I should read, and they said, "*How to Know God* by Deepak Chopra."

Then they were gone, and just as quickly, the shimmering books and gardens faded away. I was left sitting on the grass, crying. But something had changed in me—I was suddenly lighter and felt released . . . I felt childlike. I knew I was loved. I, Shere Donald, was loved!

It was clear to me now why there was cancer in my breast. You see, the breasts are the center of love and nurturing, which I'd searched my whole life for—not just from my parents or siblings, but from the world. And until that moment, I hadn't known just how much the Universe loved me . . . how much it loved everyone. Now that I'd found nurturing and love, my breast could heal—my *heart* could heal.

I went for a routine test not long after and was told that there was no longer any cancer in my breast. I was beautiful—every part of me was.

I don't "claim" breast cancer or any other disease now. It no longer defines me or grows within me. With forgiveness and love, I've released it from my body, and all tests confirm that there is no cancer regrowth.

What I do know, though, is that wellness is a journey, and I'll always have to stay focused on it to stay well. I must be consciously aware of my humanity, while still turning over the pages of my life's book. And every now and again, a past pain will surface to gently remind me that love will conquer all . . . as long as I allow it to.

(From *Transcendent Beauty,* Hay House, 2006)

Colette Baron-Reid

Deborah Samuel

Colette Baron-Reid, the author of *Remembering the Future,* is a popular spiritual intuitive, seminar leader, radio personality, motivational speaker, and musical recording artist on the EMI music label (with a top-selling meditation CD, *Journey Through the Chakras*). She has shared the stage with authors Sylvia Browne, John Holland, Caroline Myss, and many others. She currently lives in Toronto, Canada, with her husband, Marc, and their two furry children.

Website: **www.colettebaronreid.com**

SURRENDER

The event that was most pivotal in returning my gift to me was a situation that was to change me forever. I was 19 years old, and my alcoholism had progressed along with my self-centeredness—I was frozen in immaturity. I was managing my eating disorder by taking diet pills and drinking to temper their effects. By this time, I was also using street drugs on top of everything else. I was screaming inside for help, but none came.

After taking an overdose the day before final exams as a pre-law freshman in college, I went to summer school to make up for the year that I'd sabotaged. I was depressed and didn't know what to do: My intuition was blocked and muffled by all the poison I was taking into my body, and my destructiveness made it impossible to hear the warnings of my soul.

My friends on campus cautioned me to stay away from a particular bar in a seedy part of town that was rumored to attract a wilder kind of crowd. Of course, that just intrigued me more, so I went there with a friend and started hanging around. Needless to say, as a young, rebellious, curious, and self-destructive girl who was desperate for attention and not very experienced with men, I got into trouble. The place was frequented by all kinds of rough guys—drug dealers and bikers among them. I should have known better, but I'd never been exposed to this element of society before, except in the form of romanticized novels and movies.

My first taste of the dangers of that scene came one night after I insulted one of the men in front of his gang of friends. For the first time in my life, I received a violent beating at the hands of a man. His fist hit my face full on, and I flew backward over a chair and landed on the floor. I heard a crack and a hollow thud, and I must have passed out for a few seconds.

I remember picking myself up off the floor . . . the room was spinning, I could taste the blood running into my mouth, and both the front and back of my head were pounding. I'd never been hit before—I was shocked, humiliated, and very scared. No one helped me up from the floor. I'd apparently done the unthinkable, although I wasn't exactly sure what that was. . . . However, it was what happened two weeks later that would change my life forever.

I was beginning to feel cooped up in my school's dorm, where I'd remained since the incident at the bar. Still shocked by my experience, and with the bruise still evident on my face, I let my girlfriend convince me to go downtown for a beer. Later that evening we ran into a group of guys we'd seen around. I was ready to go home, but my friend wanted to stay longer, so I accepted a lift from the men. I didn't know them very well, but they seemed nice, and they'd never bothered me before.

After what had occurred two weeks earlier, I was looking for protection, so I believed them when they offered to get me home safely. Little did I know that these men had other plans for me—an experience that showed me what it was like to lose the power to choose what would happen to my own body, as well as making me truly understand the nature of shame. But the situation would also open the door to those abilities that I had previously pushed away.

The interesting thing was that the minute I accepted the ride, I knew something terrible was going to happen, but I just wasn't able to listen. My intuition was there to show me the way, but I was drunk and couldn't hear it. Although a sense of fearful expectation made my heart race, I hoped that what I anticipated was just my imagination . . . but it turned out to be all too real. Something important was indeed about to take place: I was going to be raped.

As these men violated me, I had an extraordinary and unforgettable experience. I remember it vividly, as if it were only yesterday. I saw myself being lifted out of my body, floating up to the corner of the room. I looked down at the scene below, observing what was

happening to me in a calm, detached, curious way. I remember feeling very old, as if I had been a soul since the beginning of time.

At the same time, my intuitive gift began to reveal scenes to
me from the lives of my assailants. I started to feel oddly sorry for
them. I saw a child locked in the basement without food and water,
left there by his fat, slovenly, alcoholic mother. I witnessed another
small and skinny boy being shuffled in and out of foster homes. A
third one had pale white skin and red hair and was part of a large
family—I heard yelling and screaming in a kitchen, and I saw the
father beating the mother to the floor and the little boy seething
with rage. Then I saw someone in a grocery store stealing cans of
soup and placing them in a big, unfamiliar purse with hands that
were clearly not mine.

These images swirled around me and were suspended in the
room. I also experienced a split awareness: I was conscious of
myself, and at the same time, I was able to "walk" beside my own
mind, jumping back and forth at will. Later in life, I recognized
that this is exactly the same "location" that I'm able to visit when
I read for people.

What happened to me that night left me with two distinct lega-
cies: The first was the shameful wound of rape that took many years
to heal; the second and more important one was the dual awareness
that I experienced. From that day forward, I was able to access this
awareness at will, and it ultimately became the key to my hunger
to know and understand the vastness of human consciousness and
perception. But this change for the better wasn't immediate.

For the next few years, I remained in situations that placed me
in harm's way. I was confused, and I prayed to God but believed
He would ignore me. And my mother made me promise never to
tell anyone about my experience, as she herself was a gang-rape
survivor. (During World War II, she'd been assaulted by a group of
Russian soldiers while her adopted father was forced to watch.)

I'd never wanted anyone to know about the rape. I kept it
to myself until I collapsed a month later, hemorrhaging, with a

superhigh temperature. During my subsequent stay in the hospital, I revealed the truth to my shattered parents. I was also told at the age of 19 that I'd likely never be able to bear children.

It took nine more years for me to hit bottom. The alcohol and drugs no longer provided escapes from my intuitive abilities, although the messages and visions were distorted and filtered through my damaged ego. I wore the perception of myself as a victim like a badge and made it—and my shame—the excuse for self-destruction.

I got involved in relationships with men that mirrored the abuse I'd come to expect, and I hung out with a wild group of people who partied all the time. My life became about going to clubs; staying up all night; working in bars, telemarketing offices, and retail clothing stores; and trying to make it as a singer/song-writer. However, I was failing at everything I touched. I had odd and obvious intuitive experiences that were undeniable, but I pushed them away and called them hallucinations. And I thought about suicide every day.

My intuitive gift became increasingly difficult to suppress, so I stopped trying. With 20/20 hindsight, of course, I see that I had a strong six-sensory perspective on the people around me, what they were going through, and what was about to happen. But because I was never sober, I was unable to put this to good use.

One night at a party I overheard two men talking about the fact that they'd lost their passports. One of the guys had put them in a hiding place, but when they went back to get them, they were gone. In a flash, I saw exactly who had stolen them and where they were stashed.

In my mind, I observed a Persian carpet, and looking right through it, I could "see" the passports—one of them with money in it. The next day I went to another party with my best friend at the time. While the house we were visiting was unknown to me, I immediately knew that it was the same place where the passports were hidden.

When I was introduced to the man who was hosting the party, I recognized him . . . even though I'd never met him before. Later in the evening while searching for the bathroom, I found myself in a room, where—looking down at the floor—I saw the exact carpet that I'd previously envisioned. I quickly lifted it up and found the passports, promptly gathered the stolen items, and went to let my girlfriend know what I'd found. I told her that we should give them back to their rightful owners, but she convinced me that it was none of our business. She explained that we should leave the party and never tell anyone about what I'd found in case no one believed us—because it all seemed too weird to be true.

I put the passports back, and we left the house. Yet I was bothered by my conscience afterward. I believed that I'd seen these things for the good of someone else, and I felt guilty that I hadn't returned the stolen items. My friend teased me after that by calling me "411," and she'd often tell people, "Need to know something? Go ask spooky Colette."

Around the same time, one of my pals was very much interested in tarot cards, and although she wasn't particularly intuitive, she was obsessed with reading them for herself and the people around her. I went over some of her books that dealt with the subject of connecting to the soul through objects, omens, and ritual, as well as the history of divination in different cultures. Those works spoke to me at a really deep level because I recognized the capability they described in myself.

Another friend who was a lot older than I was and was also into tarot cards bought me my first deck. I never really learned to read the cards by the book; rather, I found a way to decipher their symbols intuitively to confirm circumstances that I saw in my mind's eye. (Professionally, I still find them to be a useful tool in sessions.)

One of the cards in particular interested me more than the others—not surprisingly, it was called the Moon. Today, I recognize it as the archetype and symbol of the unseen forces in the world and human beings. The Moon is an image that represents the stirrings of the unconscious. In traditional tarot readings, it positively represents a psychic awakening that can enrich one's life; or negatively, the mystery of addiction and the consequences of a disturbed psyche. So through the tarot, the Moon and I continued our familiar and strangely compelling relationship.

My interest in tarot cards was a constant source of entertainment for myself and others, but creating music was still my priority. It was the only connection I had to something that allowed me to express myself fully, and this period was a time of prolific songwriting for me. Angst is a great fuel for poetry, and I vibrated musically to what I perceived as the deep chord of suffering in the world. It was the early '80s, and there was a lot of great music around to inspire me.

I saw myself as the wounded songstress—a secret contestant in the "Miss Victim of the World Pageant," and these feelings informed what I created. In my search for a false sense of affirmation from the world, there was something undeniable in my music that even I couldn't destroy. I used to joke about being a rock star and "making it big," but secretly I thought that success in the music business would make me a whole person, and that the accolades I dreamed of would wash away all the dirt that I believed was still stuck to me.

I'm so grateful today that nothing substantial actually happened with my career at that time because I would have become a casualty—no question about it. I don't think I could have handled the truth: The applause and the money would have done nothing to change me. I would have overdosed, or in my selfishness, committed suicide. I'm sure of that, because between the ages of 20 and 22, I tried more than once.

I knew that I was in trouble with my substance abuse long before I could stop—before I even wanted to. By the time I was 22, I was afraid of myself and my experiences. Fueled by alcohol and the unresolved pain of my past, I continued down my self-destructive path. Then I found the fast track to hell and hit rock bottom when I started smoking cocaine (it wasn't called "crack" yet). I know firsthand what it's like to be insane and to lose your self-respect, morality, and basic sense of human decency to addiction. I should have died—I came close so many times—but God had other plans for me.

Surrender

Just after Halloween in 1985, my family was devastated: We had to put our beloved dog to sleep because he had cancer and we couldn't pay the vet bills. My father had lost everything at the age of 75, and we watched a few million dollars disappear virtually overnight, along with our house and—worst of all—my dad's pride and dignity. He sat for hours staring at nothing, smoking cigarettes, and suffering from the effects of numerous strokes and the onset of Alzheimer's, while my mother cried, terrified that what little money we had left wouldn't be enough to cover expenses.

I'll always remember the night I surrendered my life to God. I'd gone to see a dealer who was giving me drugs for "free." I walked up the stairs to the bathroom and looked at myself in the mirror. For the first time, I saw myself as I really was: demoralized, bankrupt in every way, and devoid of any sense of humanity. The whites of my eyes were yellow from jaundice, my skin was puckered from dehydration, my teeth were loose, and my gums bled. I saw sores all over my body that I'd somehow neglected to notice before—including large bruises that I couldn't even remember receiving.

I'd traded everything for my addiction, and I knew I was going to die. In that moment, I recited the first honest prayer I'd said in years, and I meant it with all my heart and soul. Shaking, I held the sides of the sink with my dirty hands and cried, "Help me!"

Some may say that what happened next was just a hallucination from the drugs, but I know differently. I saw an iridescent light around me in the mirror . . . it was as if I were encased in a bubble and everything around me looked clearer. I was calm, and I knew beyond a shadow of a doubt that it was over. I was certain that I would never set foot in that drug dealer's house again. I didn't understand how, but something profound was talking to me, telling me that I'd be all right and needed to surrender—and I listened and never went back.

(From *Remembering the Future*, Hay House, 2006)

Frank H. Boehm, M.D.

Frank H. Boehm, M.D., the author of *Doctors Cry, Too,* is professor of obstetrics and gynecology, and the director of maternal/fetal medicine at Vanderbilt University School of Medicine in Nashville, Tennessee. He is also chairman of the Vanderbilt University Medical Center Ethics Committee. He is a graduate of Vanderbilt University School of Medicine and the Yale–New Haven Hospital Internship and Residency Program and is a specialist in high-risk pregnancy, called perinatology.

Dr. Boehm has three children, Todd, Tommy, and Catherine; and a granddaughter, Riley Isabel. He resides with his wife, Julie, in Nashville, Tennessee; and Boca Raton, Florida.

No Video
Camera Needed

Everywhere I go, I see people with video cameras in hand, aiming at their surroundings in an attempt, I suppose, to permanently capture the moment.

For the record, I must admit that I don't own such a camera. It's not that I have anything against modern technology; rather, it's because I believe that I already possess the best video camera there is: my eyes and my brain. After all, that's usually the only "camera" available when special moments occur.

For example, it's the eyes that capture that look of joy on your child's face when she's dancing spontaneously and rhythmically to music. Or maybe it's that last embrace with a loved one that brought tears to your eyes and a conscious, intense desire to remember all the vivid details of that moment.

I have, for example, a wonderful "tape" of a very special moment in my life. Eyes open or shut, I see it in color. I need no machine to help me play it back, and no special room to view it.

It was to be my father's last winter in Florida, the place he loved more than anywhere else. He and I had a special, loving relationship, so my visit to Fort Lauderdale during the winter holidays always brought us considerable joy. As always, I called him from my wife's family home nearby as soon as I arrived, and we agreed to meet on the beach. Being two miles apart, I was to jog south toward his home, while he would begin walking north to meet me somewhere in the middle.

As I slowly jogged past the multitude of sun worshipers and bathers, I listened to the waves and wind as well as the beautiful, mellow music piped into my ears by a small radio attached to my waist. With the sun beating down its warm, welcoming rays, I was enjoying the feeling of the sand beneath my feet and, most of all, anticipating the reunion with my dad. I was filled with happiness.

I saw him appear in the distance. His gait, so similar to mine, was unmistakable, and assured me that it was indeed my father who was approaching me on that sunny day on the beach in Lauderdale by the Sea.

And then something wonderful happened. Unable to run because of his age, he nonetheless stretched out his arms as if to embrace me, and with quicker steps than usual, pointedly made his way toward me, all the while glowing with his familiar and reassuring smile. In like manner, I stretched out my arms; and while covering the next 50 yards or so with the wind at my back, the sun in my face, and the music in my ears, I ran toward him.

My heart seemed to burst with joy. I could feel moisture in my eyes as I reached his outstretched arms, and we embraced and held each other tight. No words were spoken—there was just the sensation of our beating hearts and our swollen pride.

Suddenly, we heard applause. Other people along the beach— many my father's age—witnessed this delicious moment between father and son, and felt as moved as we did. We laughed, and arm in arm, walked to meet my mother, who eagerly awaited us.

Being trained as a physician, I am perhaps more attuned to my surroundings and aware of the body language of those I interface with, but we all have the ability to turn on our own "video camera" at those special moments. We just need practice, and the willingness to use it.

That special moment on the beach on that sunny winter day with all its vivid details is permanently imbedded in my mind. It can never be erased until I—as my beloved father did that next fall—pass away.

Thank God I had my camera with me that day.

(From *Doctors Cry, Too,* Hay House, 2001)

Joan Z. Borysenko, Ph.D.

Joan Z. Borysenko, Ph.D., is one of the leading experts on stress, spirituality, and the mind/body connection. She has a doctorate in medical sciences from Harvard Medical School; is a licensed clinical psychologist; and is the cofounder and former director of the mind/body clinical programs at the Beth Israel Deaconess Medical Center, Harvard Medical School.

Currently the president/CEO of Mind/Body Health Sciences, Inc., Joan is an internationally known speaker and consultant in women's health and spirituality, integrative medicine, and the mind/body connection. She's the author of numerous books, including the bestsellers *Minding the Body, Mending the Mind; Inner Peace for Busy People;* and *Inner Peace for Busy Women.*

Website: **www.joanborysenko.com**

MISTAKES
ARE MADE IN
LOVE'S SERVICE

My mother was a formidable woman. This story is her legacy, and a lesson about the spiritual art of forgiveness. Whenever I tell it, deep gratitude for the gift of her life takes me by surprise, as if I'm experiencing her soul face-to-face for the very first time. Part of the magic of the forgiveness we shared together is that it's always new for me, no matter how many times I tell her story. In that newness, a bit of grace often gets transmitted to those who hear or read it.

The morning of her death, in the late 1980s, my mother was transported to the basement of the hospital where I worked. She was bleeding internally, and they'd sent her down to radiology to get a fix on the source. She was gone for hours. My worried family, who had gathered in her room to say good-bye, finally sent me to search for her. I found her alone, lying on a gurney, in the hospital corridor. She'd been waiting her turn for an x-ray there, with nothing but the bare walls as a companion for several hours.

I found the doctor in charge and asked if I could take her back to her room. He shook his head from side to side, frowning. "I'm sorry, but she's bleeding," he said. "We need a diagnosis."

My mother, as pale as the sheet she was lying on, colored up a little and raised an eyebrow. "A diagnosis? Is that all you need? You mean to tell me that I've been lying here all day just because you needed a diagnosis? Why didn't you ask me?"

The doctor, who looked as if he'd just seen a ghost, was speechless for a bit. He finally stammered out a weak, "Wh-wh-what do you mean?"

"I'm dying, that's your diagnosis," my mother replied with her usual humor. To his credit, the doctor saw her point, and I was able to talk him into letting me take her back to her room. We were supposed to wait for an orderly to do the transport, but she begged me to go AWOL and speed her back to the family before anyone else could grab her. We were finally alone together in the elevator, riding back up to her floor. She looked up at me from the gurney, transparent in the way that small children and elderly people often are. There was no artifice—she was who she was. She reached for my hand, looked into my eyes, and said very simply that she'd made a lot of mistakes as a mother, and could I forgive her? The pain of a lifetime evaporated in that brief journey between floors.

I kissed her hand and then her clammy cheek. "Of course I forgive you," I whispered through a throat swollen with tears. "Can you forgive me for all the times I've judged you, for all the times I wasn't there for you? I've made a lot of mistakes as a daughter, too." She smiled and nodded at me as tears welled up in her rheumy eyes, once a striking cobalt blue more beautiful than the sky. Love built a bridge across a lifetime of guilt, hurt, and shame.

When we returned to her room, each family member had a few minutes alone with her to say good-bye. Then, as day disappeared into long shadows, and the early spring night fell like a curtain around us, everyone left except my brother, Alan; my son, Justin; and me. We three were the vigil keepers.

Justin was a young man of 20, and fiercely devoted to the grandmother who'd always been his champion. He seemed to know intuitively what a dying person needs to hear—that her life had had meaning, and that she had left the world a little bit better off by her presence. He told her stories of their good times together, of how her love had sustained him. Justin held his dying grandmother in his arms, sang to her, prayed for her, and read to her for much of her last night with us. I was so proud of him.

Unusual things can happen at births and deaths. The veil between this world and the next is thin at these gateways, as souls enter and leave. Around midnight, Mom fell into a final morphine-assisted sleep. Justin and I were alone with her while my brother took a break. We were meditating on either side of her bed. But I was awake, not asleep; perfectly lucid, not dreaming. The world seemed to shift on its axis, and I had a vision, which if you've ever had one, you know seems realer than real. This life appears to be the dream, and the vision a glimpse of a deeper reality.

In the vision, I was a pregnant mother, laboring to give birth. I was also the baby being born. It was an odd, and yet a deeply familiar, experience to be one consciousness present in two bodies. With a sense of penetrating insight and certainty, I realized that there's only one consciousness in the entire universe. Despite the illusion of separateness, there's only one of us here, and that One is the Divine.

As the baby moved down the birth canal, my consciousness switched entirely into its tiny body. I felt myself moving down the dark tunnel. It was frightening, a death of sorts, as I left the watery darkness of the womb to travel through this unknown territory. I emerged quite suddenly into a place of perfect peace, complete comfort, and ineffable Light of the sort that people tell about in near-death experiences.

The Light is beyond any kind of description. No words can express the total love, absolute forgiveness, tender mercy, Divine bliss, complete reverence, awesome holiness, and eternal peace that the Light is. That Light of Divine love seemed to penetrate my soul. I felt as though it had seen and known my every thought, motive, action, and emotion in this life. In spite of my obvious shortcomings and terrible errors, it held me in absolute gentleness, complete forgiveness, and unconditional love as you would a small child. I knew beyond question, cradled in the Light, that love is who we are and what we are becoming.

Scenes of my mother and me together flashed by. Many of these scenes were of difficult times when our hearts were closed to one another and we were not in our best selves. Yet, from the vantage point of the Light, every interaction seemed perfect, calculated to teach us something about loving better. As the scenes went on, life's mysterious circularity came clear. Mom had birthed me into this world, and I had birthed her soul back out. We were one. I was reborn at the moment of her death—bathed in love, forgiveness, and gratitude. I thought of the words of St. Paul, that we see through a glass, darkly. For a moment I was granted the gift of seeing face-to-face.

When I opened my eyes, the entire room was bathed in light. Peace was like a palpable presence, a velvety stillness, the essence of Being. All things appeared to be interconnected, without boundaries. I remembered how my high-school chemistry teacher had explained that everything was made of energy, of light. That night I could see it. Everything was part of a whole, pulsing with the Light of Creation. I looked across my mother's dead body and saw my son sitting opposite me. Justin's face was luminous. It looked as though he had a halo. He was weeping softly, tears like diamonds glinting with light. I got up and walked around the bed, pulling a chair up close to him. He looked deep into my eyes and asked softly whether I could see that the room was filled with light. I nodded, and we held hands in the silence. After a few beats, he whispered reverently that the light was his grandma's last gift. "She's holding open the door to eternity so that we can have a glimpse," he told me.

Continuing to look deeply into my eyes, Justin spoke from a well of wisdom deeper than his 20 years. "You must be so grateful to your mother," he said. I knew exactly what he meant. I'd been an ungrateful daughter, holding on to years of grudges against my difficult mom. Now my heart was overflowing with gratitude, which was a completely new emotion with respect to her.

It turned out that Justin had also had a vision, which to this day he has kept to himself. But he told me these things there in the hospital room where the shell of his beloved grandmother's 81-year-old body lay. My mother, he said, was a great soul, a wise being who had far more wisdom than her role in this lifetime had allowed her to express. She had taken a role much smaller than who she was, he assured me, so that I would have someone to resist. In resisting her, I would have to become myself. My purpose in life, he explained—a purpose in which she had played a vital part—was to share the gift of what I'd learned about healing, compassion, God, and self-discovery.

I looked down at the floor to gather myself, and then back into my son's gentle green eyes. "Can you forgive me, Justin? I know I've made a lot of mistakes as a mother. Do you know how much I love you?"

He took my hand. "Mistakes are made in love's service," he whispered.

And then the energy in the room shifted, the Light faded, and we hugged for a long time. Finally breaking away, he smiled and laughed, "Hey, Mom, you wounded me in just the right ways."

We got up and did a silly little dance together that we saw Ren and Stimpy, the cartoon characters, do one day on television. "Happy Happy Joy Joy!" we chanted as we danced around incongruously in the room of a dead mother, a dead grandmother, whose love we had shared and experienced in very different ways.

"Please remember that you forgive me, sweetheart, " I reminded Justin a little while later. "I'm sure that I'm not done making mistakes yet."

In the 20-plus years since we shared my mother's death, Justin and I have both made mistakes, and we've both taken responsibility for them and made amends as best we could. But the grace of mother-child forgiveness, and the sense that we're here together because we're learning to love, has made the process much easier. For that alone, I'm so very grateful.

(From *Inner Peace for Busy Women,* Hay House, 2003)

Gregg Braden

Melissa Sherman

New York Times best-selling author **Gregg Braden** has been a featured guest at international conferences and on media specials, exploring the role of spirituality in technology. From his groundbreaking book *Awakening to Zero Point*, to his pioneering work in *Walking Between the Worlds* and the controversy of *The Isaiah Effect*, *The God Code*, and *The Divine Matrix*, Gregg ventures beyond the traditional boundaries of science and spirituality, offering meaningful solutions to the challenges of our time.

Website: **www.greggbraden.com**

My Friend Merlin

Some of my most compelling relationships have been with animals. One week in the early 1990s, I was leading a combination workshop and retreat at an inn in Mount Shasta, California. A tiny black kitten wandered down the hallways of the inn, found his way into my room and my heart, and never left.

My newfound friend had been born about five weeks earlier to a young female cat that had never given birth before and could not nurse her litter. By the time the employees at the inn discovered what had happened, they believed that all of the kittens had died. A few days later, however, a small miracle occurred. The mother cat emerged from her hiding place carrying a tiny heap of bones and fur that had survived all that time without food! Immediately the staff began to nurse the tiny kitten back to health. Acknowledging his magical strength and sheer will to survive, they named him Merlin.

Finding my room that evening, Merlin purred and meowed at the door until I surrendered to my urge to care for every animal on the entire planet and let him in. During the week of the program, he slept with me each night and sat with me each morning as I ate breakfast in my room. He would watch me shave from the edge of the bathroom sink and walk across my 35-millimeter slides (in the days *before* PowerPoint!) as I prepared them for the next day. Every morning he would stand on the edge of the bathtub as I showered and catch droplets of water in his mouth as they bounced from my body. By the end of the week, Merlin and I were good friends, and I found myself tremendously attached to the little miracle with such a will to live.

Through a series of synchronicities that soon occurred, Merlin and I found ourselves on a cross-country journey to my home in the high desert of northern New Mexico. He quickly became my "family," and for the next three years he was with me each evening while I prepared dinner, and he napped beside my ancient Apple computer while I wrote my first book.

One night Merlin went outside, as he always did at that time of the evening, and I never saw him again. It was in the summer of 1994, during the week when a massive comet was impacting Jupiter. At first I thought that maybe he'd just gone exploring and I'd see him again soon. It may have been that Merlin navigated through the desert using the magnetic lines of the earth, as birds and whales do—the same fields that were upset by Jupiter's strange effect on Earth's magnetic fields. These could have shifted and led him somewhere else. Or it may have been for a host of other reasons. The fact was that Merlin was gone.

When two days passed and I didn't see him, I began to search for him. I took no phone calls and did absolutely no business for nearly a week as I scoured the fields north of Taos, New Mexico. Was he caught in a trap that the ranchers had set for the coyotes that hunted their sheep? Maybe he was stuck in an old building or a well and couldn't get out. For days I searched owls' nests and looked in every badger burrow and coyote den that I could find. Finally, I stopped looking for Merlin and began looking for traces of him: his fur or his collar. All my efforts were fruitless.

One morning as I was lying in bed just before sunrise in a dreamy, half-awakened state, I simply asked for a sign. I needed to know what had happened to my friend. Before I'd even finished the question in my mind, something happened that had never occurred before and has never happened since. From the loft in my home, I heard a sound coming from outside, then another, and then another. Within seconds, coming from every direction, completely encircling the property, I heard the unmistakable cry of coyotes—more than I'd ever heard in all the years I'd lived on that property.

For what seemed like minutes, they yipped and howled until just as suddenly as they began, they stopped. I had tears in my eyes as I said out loud, "I don't think Merlin is with me any longer." In that moment, I was shown what had happened to my friend. I knew that the coyotes had taken him and that I would never see him again.

Later the same day, I began to see coyotes all over the property—in broad daylight! Certainly I'd seen them in the past, yet always before, they'd appeared at sunset or just before sunrise. Today, they were everywhere in the middle of the afternoon—single ones, two or three together, young pups and families, all casually strolling through the fields.

Here is the reason why I offer this story. The loss of Merlin hurt me. In my pain, I could have gone after each coyote, one by one, thinking that "this is the one" that took my friend. I could have stood high on the top of a farm building with a rifle in my hands and avenged Merlin's death until there were no coyotes left in the entire valley. I could have done all that . . . and nothing would have changed. Merlin would still be gone.

I wasn't angry at the coyotes; I just missed my friend. I missed his personality and the funny sounds that he made as he stalked the "big game" like the moths on the screen door at night. I missed the way he looked at me upside down while lying on the cool tile floors in the summer.

That afternoon I began driving along the dusty gravel road that weaves its way through the valley to the highway. It was on this drive that I had my first experience of blessing. As I rolled up the windows so that no one would hear me (not that there was anyone within miles of me anyway!), I blessed Merlin in his passing, acknowledging him and all the joy that he brought to my life. That was the easy part. Then I began to bless the coyotes, especially the ones that took his life. Before long, I actually began to feel an odd sort of kinship with them. I knew that what had happened was not an intentional act to hurt me. They simply did what coyotes do! I blessed myself in trying to make sense of why nature sometimes seems so cruel.

At first nothing seemed to happen. I was so hurt that I couldn't let the blessing "in." Within a couple of repetitions, however, the change began. The feeling started as warmth in my stomach that swelled as it spread throughout my body in all directions. As my eyes welled with tears, I found myself gasping big sobs. I pulled to the side of the road and did my best to bless until there was no energy to bless anymore. I knew, for that day, that the blessing was complete.

The thing about the act of blessing is that the world doesn't change; we're the only ones who do! In our willingness to acknowledge and release whatever it is that's hurt us, the world looks different and we become stronger, healthier people.

Interestingly, following the peace that I made with the coyotes that day, although I hear them at night, I've never seen another one cross my property line. Last year, however, I did see another cat of a different kind: my very first mountain lion. And she'd crossed under the fence line to come right into my backyard!

(From *Secrets of the Lost Mode of Prayer,* Hay House, 2006)

Jim Brickman

Kevin Merrill

Jim Brickman's Grammy-nominated dazzling piano artistry and clever songwriting skills have led to sales of more than six million albums, gold- and platinum-selling recordings, hit PBS concert specials, a weekly syndicated radio show, and several chart-topping songs. In theaters across the country, Jim turns a simple concert stage into an intimate space where imagination takes off, using musical notes to weave a tapestry of emotion, color, and spirit. He's the author (with Cindy Pearlman) of *Simple Things* and *Love Notes*.

I Love Vanilla!

When I was in advertising, I was working on a commercial for a top burger chain that I can't mention, because I don't need any calls from their lawyers.

Anyway, I walked into this editing session, and all the ad people were having this huge yelling and screaming match, because for their commercial, the pickles weren't big enough, the burger looked a bit small in comparison to the tomato slices, and if some genius didn't fix it, then for God's sake, the onions would be really overwhelming. I bit my lip so as not to laugh, but my impulse to chuckle was short-lived, because I then heard a few words I'll never forget.

Some blowhard yelled, "And the music sounds like something Elmer Fudd wrote in his spare time!"

Yes, it's okay to feel my pain. I can still remember that feeling. It's when your stomach drops a few hundred feet, your heart starts doing an internal mambo, and your head begins to ache, even though you're not the type to get migraines.

But the insults didn't stop there. The same putz went on to say, "The music is too cute. This isn't a cartoon!"

The ad people were ruthless. My theory is that they're so "up front" because they really would rather be writing music or books, but their fancy offices and designer ties seem to give them a license to wield their frustration as a superpower. They're the kryptonite to your Superman. And if any ad execs are reading this book, I'm sorry. Of course, I don't mean *you*. Just your colleagues.

When I first started writing jingles, I often heard these words: "Jim, we really hate this!" Actually, in many ways, it helped me. Every bit of rejection added a sort of Teflon coating to me. It's true what they say about developing a thick skin. Now if I walk in to my record label, I'll look around the room at these music bigwigs and say, "Hi, you guys. When I say this, I'm actually serious—tell me what you think of this song."

There are a few bits of encouragement I can pass on here. And I say this from my heart.

First of all, if you're rejected, please don't give up on your dream. I had a friend who was a photography student at a major university. She was a great photographer, but a certain "top" professor simply didn't like women. He gave her a tough time all semester, until she ultimately changed her major to business. She completely gave up and allowed one opinion to crush a lifelong dream.

If I had given up every time someone told me I'd never make music professionally, I'd probably be sitting in some ad exec's office today, hearing, "Your music makes the hot dog feel less significant than the mustard."

Singer Richard Marx was turned down by 12 record companies before he had an international hit record. Sylvester Stallone was told by most of the major studios that *Rocky* was a dumb idea for a movie and no one would ever go see it. It won an Oscar for the best picture of 1976.

The point is, there is no right and wrong—it's all up to interpretation. You may like licorice; I can't stand it. You may like Madonna; I'm not into her. I like sweet; you may like salty. Fruity, forget it—but I know there are people who savor those sour-apple candies. Give me chocolate M&Ms.

But it's still cool that there's a variety of foods that will clog your arteries and ruin your teeth. Obviously, everyone has different tastes. And someone rejecting you on any level—professional, personal, or snack food–wise—can be dealt with in a simple way. They don't share your same tastes. Period.

Some people at my record company are always on me. They'll say, "Jim, we think you need a hipper image. We don't really like hearing you tell the story onstage about how you learned to play piano on a piece of felt before your mother could afford to buy you a real instrument."

So I changed my act. I started skipping the felt story. Then after the shows, I'd be talking to fans backstage, and over and over again, I'd hear, "It was a great show, but how come you didn't tell the felt story? I told my husband, 'Wait till you hear this part about how he learned to play music.'"

In everyone's life, you'll hear, "Well, we just don't like such and such." I suggest you hit these cynics with a simple response. Just say, "Okay, what would you prefer?" I bet you'll hear these words, "Well, I dunno." And then say back to them, "Well, until you do know, I'll continue to do it my way."

You can be rejected for so many things: You're a bad cook or a sloppy kisser, which brings me to critics, whom I've saved for the end of this story. Talk about rejection. I've read: "Jim's music is so syrupy." Or this is a good one: I recently got slammed by a journalist (of course, my mom cut the review out of the paper and sent it to me). Suffice it to say, it wasn't kind, because the scribe wrote: "Jim Brickman does the most vanilla music I've ever heard in my life."

I'm like, *I love vanilla!* I put vanilla in everything. I even put it in my protein shakes. I have vanilla candles. I know a lot of people who love vanilla, too.

My take was that it wasn't a criticism of me—it was an endorsement for vanilla lovers everywhere. . . .

(From *Simple Things,* Hay House, 2001)

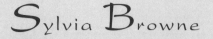

Sylvia Browne

E. Chris Wisner

Sylvia Browne is the #1 *New York Times* best-selling author and world-famous psychic medium who appears regularly on the *Montel Williams Show* and *Larry King Live,* as well as making countless other media and public appearances. With her down-to-earth personality and great sense of humor, Sylvia thrills audiences on her lecture tours—and she's still found the time to write a number of immensely popular books, including *Secrets & Mysteries of the World, If You Could See What I See,* and *Exploring the Levels of Creation.* Sylvia lives in Northern California and plans to write as long as she can.

Website: **www.sylvia.org**

My Heaven
Is Right Here

I learn about life, not only from my own experiences, but also from others, so I'd like to tell you about Sister Francis, as well as some other folks.

About 40 years ago I was working at St. Albert the Great, teaching second grade. Sister Francis was a fellow instructor, and we'd try to spend our free time between classes or at lunch together. That always meant going outdoors, because Sister Francis dearly loved to be out in nature. She and I would go out rain or shine, and she never failed to say, "What a beautiful day this is! Look at the splendor God has laid out before us!"

At first I thought she was exaggerating, but gradually I began to see what she saw: the variances in temperature, the cloud formations, the soft beat of the rain, and even the cold that made your face pink and flushed when you came back inside. Sister Francis truly had heaven in her own mind.

Then there was my grandfather, Marcus Coil, who'd become a millionaire in Springfield, Missouri, by starting up some of the town's first laundries and mercantile stores. By the time the family had moved to Kansas City, however, he'd lost every penny in the stock market. Although it was during the time of the Great Depression, every day my grandfather would press his now-shiny-with-wear suit and shirt (which Grandma Ada had to keep repairing the frayed cuffs on) and sit in the waiting room of Pacific Gas and Electric looking for work. And every day, the head of the company would come out and say, "Sorry, Marcus, we have nothing for you today."

For one year my grandfather followed this routine. Finally, the CEO told my grandpa that he was sick of seeing him every day and that anyone who had that type of perseverance deserved a job. My grandfather was given a menial position, but in six months he became the head of the whole district office. He kept telling Grandma Ada, "I made it once; I know how to do it again." Was this all about money? God, no—it was about providing for his family and taking a positive and undaunted attitude. My grandfather was able to create a heaven out of his hell.

On the other side of this coin you have my mother. It's hard to understand how she could have come from the same family as my wonderful grandparents, her brother Marcus (who had cerebral palsy but was an angel on Earth whom everyone called "Brother"), and her brother Paul, who was also psychic and used to talk to God daily before he died of cancer at the age of 21. Yup, out of this family of beloved people came my mother. I used to obsess about not liking her until my spirit guide Francine told me many years later, "You can only honor your parents if they are honorable."

My mother was not only abusive physically, but her greatest forte was to try to damage her family members with mental abuse. I was too tall, not pretty, and too strong willed. But *I* thought I was smart, even when she told me I wasn't—and this seemed to set a fire in my gut to make her wrong. I was also my father's favorite, which endeared me to her even less.

Now I could have wilted under her abuse and become like her, but instead, I went under my beloved grandma's wing and basked in the light of my dad's approval. My poor sister, Sharon, wasn't so fortunate, however: My mother got her claws into her and for a time controlled her and almost made her an invalid. To this day, my mother's influence has affected my sister's life—and not in a positive way. (You can say that I was stronger, and that may be so, but I also chose my chart.)

Being psychic didn't help me in my mother's eyes, even though she'd grown up with a psychic mother, brother, grandmother, and uncle. With all due respect, she may have had enough of it, but instead of encouraging me as Grandma Ada did, when I was ten years old, she told me, "Keep this spooky thing up and I'll have you locked up." I can remember being so frightened that night that I could hear my heart beat through the bed, and I truly prayed that my gifts would disappear.

When I hesitantly told my grandmother about the incident, I remember her listening carefully and getting a grim look on her face. She silently put on her coat and grabbed my hand, and we both marched off to see my mother. Now this was one of only two times I saw my grandmother get angry in the 18 years that I was with her. Seething with anger, she went up to my mother, put her face close to hers, and said, "Celeste, if you ever say that to Sylvia again, I'll personally see to it that *you* are locked up!" So that ended that . . . except for the constant snorts and sighs of disapproval my mother directed toward me over the years whenever I'd do mini readings for friends or come out with a zinger of psychic insight.

My psychic ability was even accepted by my childhood friends (who will attest to it). In fact, I recently attended my 50th high-school reunion, and my classmates all told me they were proud of me. Even the nuns and priests, believe it or not, were good to me back then—while they didn't always understand how I knew what I knew, they never condemned me. In fact, all throughout Catholic high school and college, and even during the 18 years that I taught in Catholic schools, I was never made to feel that I was evil or an oddity. At Presentation High School in San Jose, California, they even let me teach world religions, which I have to confess had Gnosticism on the agenda more than the Bible, Bhagavad Gita, Koran, or the Talmud. Of course I gave time to all of these, but I kept coming back to a loving God and the fact that life is what we make of it inside our soul . . . because, after all, that's where our heaven and hell reside.

Getting back to my childhood, as I grew into my late teens, my father was making $3,000 a month. That was a fortune in those days, so I didn't have an underprivileged upbringing in those years, but I truly would have foregone that for a semblance of a happy home. Yet I can honestly say that I was happy overall because I had the rest of my family and my friends. I chose to

41

respect my mother, while at the same time putting her on a shelf in the back of my mind.

During this time, my grandmother fell on hard times. My grandfather had died, and Grandma Ada was taking care of Brother. It's very difficult for me to relive this portion of my memories, for my mother stuck them both in a literal flophouse. You may wonder why my father didn't intervene, but it's more unbelievable and complex than that. My father left everything to my mother to handle because he traveled all the time and really didn't know what was going on with my mother's family. I was right there when she lied and told him that no one would take Brother in because of his cerebral palsy. Well, she never even looked—nor was she about to spend any of her considerable allowance to have her family members taken care of.

I remember the day Grandma Ada and Brother moved into a three-flight walk-up that my mother had put them in. Brother was afraid of stairs because his disease threw his balance off, and then a drunk came out brandishing a knife. I think I was so full of grief that I turned on the man and screamed, "Get back in your room before I use that knife on you!" He looked befuddled and stunned. I guess so . . . seeing a 13-year-old girl going into what looked like a manic fit.

I saw that my beloved family members were going to be reduced to living in a dirty one-room flat with a communal bathroom down the hall. I kept thinking, *Please, God, let me grow up fast so that I can take care of them.* The room contained a bed, one straight-back chair, two hot plates, a few large windows with no curtains, a small sink, and a dresser—and that was it. (Oh, except for the two dishes, glasses, and sets of eating utensils; along with a pair of sheets and a flimsy blanket, plus two pillows and towels that my extravagant mother had so thoughtfully provided.) This is what my grandmother—who was of German nobility, escaped the war, gave to charity, healed the sick, and helped as many people as she could—had been given by her own daughter.

Grandma Ada sat down on the chair, and for a moment I saw what looked like a cloud cross her china blue eyes. But then she threw her hat on the bed and sat down. Then, like my granddaughter, Angelia, still does, I flung myself on my grandmother's lap—all 13 years of me. She must have seen my pain because she said, "Look at those windows! Brother can look out every day and see the sights, and we'll have light all day long." She patted me and said, "It'll be just fine, darling. I'll make it great in no time."

I'd like to take a moment here to talk a little bit more about Brother, who lived with my grandmother until her death at age 88. He was one of the most brilliant people I've ever known. He read everything—history, religion, politics, you name it—and could talk about it. He was very frail, with reddish hair and blue eyes, and stood only about 5'8". His head was tilted to one side because of his cerebral palsy, and his neck would bob violently when he was agitated or nervous. When I walked down the street with him and people stared (as they're wont to do), I glared at them, silently daring them to say one word.

When she was asked about how hard it was to take care of him, my grandmother, without hesitation, would say, "Are you kidding? Look what joy and company I have in my older years—we have fun, read, talk, and laugh; and without him, I'd be alone. How can this blessing be a burden?" Once again, as you can see, out of a hell (or what's perceived to be one) lies a heaven in disguise.

My grandmother never really psychically read for me because we couldn't for each other, but she did say that I'd have two boys, would go to California, and that people would know my name. "Me, a girl from Missouri? I think not! And how will they know my name?" I pressed her.

She replied, "You'll carry the torch that was built upon itself for 300 years." *How poetic,* I'd think, but then I rationalized that she loved me so much she was blinded by it. In fact, in a half-kidding way, I once asked her while we were cooking, "Grandma, how much do you love me?"

She stopped what she was doing, looked at me, and said, "My heart would hear you and beat if it lay for a century dead." Now try to top that one!

My grandmother was a writer, too, and someday I'm going to publish her letters. Each one is filled with quotes, all of which were gloriously optimistic. She *always* made a heaven out of a living hell. For example, in that room that she and Brother shared, she got ahold of some donated fabric and made a skirt for the dresser and one for the sink to hide the utensils and dishes, and she made another sheet for the bed . . . but it was still a rattrap.

When my father came home two weeks later, I immediately went to him and tried to explain how awful it was. He had some business issue on his mind, so I could tell he wasn't with me. My mother came in and said, "Bill, don't listen to her—she's always so dramatic anyway. You can go see for yourself what a cozy place it is," knowing full well that he wouldn't. He either wanted to believe her or was afraid not to, I'll never know. I do know that after that, he'd slip me money to take to Grandma.

I can remember on more than one occasion skipping school with money in my pocket, taking the streetcar in the blinding snow to 18th and Baltimore, and walking up to that damn run-down building. I'd look up and see a form in the window, standing there with that Gibson-girl hairstyle she had, smiling and waving because she psychically knew that I was coming (after all, she had no phone). I'd climb the steps and give her the money, prompting her to clap her hands together, tell me what a good man my father was, and remark that we were going to have a feast. That meant a soda, cheese, milk, and hamburger stew.

As painful as it was, Grandma could even light up a dingy cell-like room with love and joy. She'd always say, "Isn't this cozy?" or "Aren't we lucky?" or "Aren't we happy to have each other?" I decided to believe her. And it didn't take long for people to again find out where she was. Long lines began to form to see her—priests, laypeople, old people, and sick people . . . she'd see everyone.

I used to say, "God, please let me just be one-tenth as strong, brave, and positive as she is throughout *my* life."

Well, I won't lie or be humble, but I can't honestly say that I've arrived at the point that my grandparents or Sister Francis reached, but I try valiantly. I *can* say that when I got divorced from my abusive first husband, Gary, and was relegated to tenement living (where there was algae all over the pool in back), I told my boys that it was just water lilies. However, after two ear infections, I decided that enough was enough.

Not only did I have Paul and Chris, I also had my adopted daughter, Mary, whose mother had simply given her to me when the child was only 6. (Mary left us when she was 22 and is now married with two girls and living near Boston.) And I was so strung out at the time with my ex-husband's threats to kill us that I didn't know if I was coming or going. The police actually told me that Gary could stand on the sidewalk in a threatening manner and there was nothing I could do about it. One officer said that the only way I could stop him would be to pull him into our apartment and shoot him. Since I could never ever hurt anyone or anything in that way, that wasn't a viable option either.

Yet, even through this horrendous period, the kids and I managed to scrape by. People were so caring. For example, when Chris had a terrible earache (the attack of the "water lilies"), the woman next door came over with what I deem were no less than magical drops for his ear—and he was fine from then on. Mary was a love, and together, even at her age, we'd laugh about all the pork and beans we ate.

At this same time, my mother went to a lawyer to try to get my children. My lawyer was flabbergasted: Here I was, a Catholic schoolteacher and a good mother, and she was going after custody with my ex-husband. The reason, she explained later, was that she didn't want to lose us. *Huh?*

At one point in my late 20s and early 30s, as I was raising the kids by myself, teaching school, doing readings, *and* attending classes, I began to see that my life wasn't going the way I wanted it to. It felt like an endless circle of readings, teaching, raising children, school, and nothing else. Then I began to ask myself, "What do *you* want, Sylvia?"

I really wanted to teach and help people, but I also needed to give the children a good home. So I quit my job as a schoolteacher and opened my foundation. We had two rooms and taught classes in the evenings, and I brought my kids with me. They'd sit in the back and do their homework—then we'd go to Denny's, eat dinner, and talk about everything. Sure, finances were really tough, but the trade-off was great. It was the process of selection: I had my family with me because when they were in school I did readings in my home, and three nights a week, they went with me to lectures or classes.

Life went on and on . . . it can take on a Shakespearean quality (or even a comedy of errors), but you roll with it. Life also gives you grief and sorrow in large measures: It can deceive and disappoint you, but it also gives you happiness; ecstasy; satisfaction; loving friends, pets, and family—all part of the montage that makes your life how you perceive it: a joy.

When my third husband, Larry, exited several years ago, things became quite difficult. I like having partnership at this point in my life, but I also feel that people my age or even younger should find fulfillment by doing what they feel is right, not what society dictates. Anyway, right in the middle of the divorce, Dal Brown (my second husband whose name I still carry, although I added an *e* to it) showed up at my office and told me that he was getting an amicable divorce from his wife of two years. He was working as a store manager in Auburn, California, and had come to the Bay Area on business when he decided out of the blue to stop by and see me. His children had moved away, and we talked about old times. We'd kept in touch sporadically since our divorce, and one thing led to another. . . .

Although Dal has had many serious health problems (including heart trouble and several operations that left him on disability for a while), shortly after both our divorces were final we decided to become companions for one another. After all, I'd known him for almost 40 years, and we had 18 years of marriage together. All the old hurts were forgotten—what he'd done with our finances had been out of stupidity, not malicious intent. So we're friends . . . and even though he doesn't share any part of my business, it's nice to have someone around who knows me. He has his life and I have mine, but we try to spend as much time as we can with each other.

As you can see, with the closing of one door, another opens. Even though I was hurt by my last divorce, I found solace in the fact that there was so much good in my life. These days, my perfect setting is coming home from being on the road and sitting next to the fireplace with my granddaughter, Angelia, needlepointing and talking, while my grandson, Willy, plays with his toy trucks, with a stew on the stove that we can eat whenever we want.

And then I feel all the loved ones who have passed over—Dad, Grandma Ada, and Brother; my dear friend Dr. Small, who was always there for me if I couldn't pay the medical bills for my children; Bob Williams, my mentor, friend, and teacher whom I dearly loved; Joe, who was one of my first loves; Abass, who was my friend and tour guide in Egypt (and when I was going through my last divorce would call me every day and ask, "How are you doing, Queenie?"—his nickname for me); and myriad other souls who have passed on. I know that they're all there with Francine and the angels, and the room fills up with love.

That's when I tell myself, "This is your heaven right here, Sylvia."

(From *If You Could See What I See,* Hay House, 2006)

Peter Calhoun

Toby Foster

Peter Calhoun, the author of *Soul on Fire*, is a former Episcopal priest who has followed the path of modern shamanism for nearly four decades. He is currently traveling throughout the United States for book signings, lectures, and workshops on the subjects of shamanism, healing, and personal empowerment.

In addition, Peter offers an apprenticeship program for in-depth studies of modern shamanism. He and his partner, Astrid, are cofounders of an international Alliance for Spiritual Ecology. During the warm seasons, they take groups of adults out into wilderness areas for vision questing.

Website: **www.petercalhoun.com**

LITTLE DOVE

Although we had known each other for several years and had recently been married, Astrid and I were still caught up in the euphoria of sharing time together in the natural world that we so deeply loved and revered. We left early one morning for a trip to the nearby Smoky Mountains. We took about 20 single-gallon plastic jugs to fill with water from a natural spring used by local people for drinking water.

It was one of those halcyon days in the foothills; the calm late August day had a hint of fall in the air. The serenity of the place was conducive to a sense of lightheartedness and abandon. I was remembering an extraordinary experience I had ten years ago with a dove. While driving down a country road one day, a dove had flown into my windshield. Feeling sick with grief, I pulled over and said a prayer for the spirit of the dove. I asked that it be healed of the trauma of its death and be guided on its return to its source. I blessed it, sending my love to this being whose life I had unintentionally taken.

Then a most unexpected thing happened. An ocean of love that rolled in like an invisible tide enveloped me. I had no idea where this love came from, but I knew that the love I had sent out had been reciprocated. Throughout the day, I basked in the wonderful energy. The dove I thought I had lost had become more alive to me than ever in this tidal force of unconditional love that understandably had come from the spirit of all Doves.

This morning was the first time in years I had thought of that experience. At the time I failed to see that it was a premonition of another remarkable encounter with a dove. Once our jugs were filled, Astrid and I waded out to the middle of the shallow river, whose crystal-clear waters flow out of the Great Smoky Mountains less than ten miles away.

Wading in a cold mountain stream is an effective tool for stopping one's internal dialogue. Once our mental chatter is at rest, we automatically shift to the spiritual mind, usually without our notice. Our inherent magical consciousness is an aspect of this spiritual mind. I have observed that even wild animals lose their instinctive fear of us when we have shifted into this magical state.

While we were standing in the river's cooling waters, we were captivated by a school of minnows, so perfectly reflected in the sunlight that they appeared as a cluster of sparkling diamonds submerged just beneath the surface of the waters. The image brought us into an awareness of the sacredness of this special place.

Finally, refreshed and in a state of quietude, we stepped out of the water onto a grassy clearing. I had walked to some bushes to relieve myself while Astrid began walking to our car. No sooner had she taken a few steps than a wild dove flew out of the nearby trees landing next to her feet. Although it flew well, she could see that it was a juvenile. She wondered if it simply did not see her, although this seemed unlikely. Excitedly, Astrid called me over to witness this bizarre scenario.

We were as still as mice, fearful of startling it. Unafraid, the dove walked over and began pecking at the ground only inches away from us. Then, to our astonishment, it climbed on top of my tennis shoe and began pulling at my shoelaces with its beak. We were enthralled.

Curious, we backed away to see what it would do—only to find that it followed us. We backed up several times with the same results. The crazy little dove thought he belonged to us.

Wondering how far we could take this, we walked about 20 paces away to see its reaction. At first the little dove didn't seem to know where we'd gone, but as soon as it heard our voices, it flew over to us. Then, as if to say, "You are my territory!" it climbed on Astrid's shoe. We continued to look on in disbelief.

This was just too much! We had become enraptured with the little dove that was following us around like a puppy. Finally, I cautiously reached down and picked it up, placing it on Astrid's head, certain it would fly away. Instead, the dove began pulling on her hair with its beak. Then, as if pleased with its new residence, it settled down to nest in her hair.

Unfortunately, by now it was time for us to leave. This was easier said than done. Even when we opened the car door, the dove did not flinch. Apparently, it was committed to remaining in its new home. The little dove had quickly endeared itself to us by its strange attachment to us and the hilarious act of nesting in Astrid's hair.

We hesitated before actually entering our car to see what choice the dove would make. For a few moments more it remained motionless, watching us. But then its natural instinct must have overridden the strange kinship it felt with us because it flapped its wings once and effortlessly flew away.

We were enthralled by the magic of this experience, but as I pondered what had happened, I felt that there was still something we had missed. I knew that many times in her past Astrid had taken in sick or wounded birds, nursing them back to health. In fact, as recently as six months ago, she had attempted to heal a dying pigeon. It struck me that all these events were somehow related. Could it be that somehow her compassionate acts had bound her to the group soul of doves and pigeons and perhaps I'd become bound as well?

Together we witnessed how our acts of compassion for wild creatures had gone full circle and come back to reward us for such love and caring. From such experiences, I've learned that there are invisible threads that span both time and space to connect us in mysterious ways to life in its infinite diversity.

This wondrous experience with the little dove demonstrated to both Astrid and me that undreamed-of possibilities exist in our relationship with Creation. This experience was one of ecstatic joy for us. Our attempt to quiet our minds and blend with the natural world around us was rewarded by this extraordinary visitation.

We perceived that by developing these simple disciplines, it was possible to heal the ancient rift between the human and animal worlds. How enriched our lives can become when we shift from our existential separation into an ecstatic oneness with life around us!

(From *Soul on Fire*, Hay House, 2007)

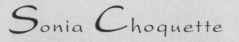

Sonia Choquette

John Reilly

Sonia Choquette is a world-renowned author, storyteller, vibrational healer, and six-sensory spiritual teacher in international demand for her guidance, wisdom, and capacity to heal the soul. She's the author of eight best-selling books, including *Diary of a Psychic* and *Trust Your Vibes,* and numerous audio programs and card decks. Sonia was educated at the University of Denver and the Sorbonne in Paris, and holds a Ph.D. in metaphysics from the American Institute of Holistic Theology. She resides with her family in Chicago.

Website: **www.soniachoquette.com**

A SPELL OF
GOOD LUCK

When I was still in the third grade, I experienced a dramatic shift in my psychic sensibilities. I didn't just *feel* what people thought, I actually began to hear it in my head, which was disconcerting and exciting at the same time.

One day as I was more or less daydreaming at my desk, I heard my teacher Sister Mary Margaret's voice say, "I'm going to give these kids a surprise spelling bee tomorrow. That will keep them on their toes."

Astounded to hear her voice so clearly, I snapped straight up in my chair, wondering if she'd spoken out loud and I'd just missed it. She noticed my abrupt jolt and the surprised expression on my face and studied me for a moment, frowning and suspicious. "Sonia, what are you up to?"

"Nothing," I said, feeling guilty at eavesdropping on her thoughts and fearful she'd know, because Sister Mary Margaret was an irritable nun prone to hitting you on the head whenever she felt like it, which was often.

She continued to eye me suspiciously while I concentrated on my desk. Then she said crossly, "Quit daydreaming and get back to work."

Her harsh tone made me shudder and surprised the other kids, who stared at me, wondering what was going on. I was normally Miss Goody Two-shoes, who never, ever got reprimanded. Excited at hearing my teacher's voice in my head, and even more excited about what I'd heard, I couldn't help but want to tell someone; it was too big to keep to myself. So I told my friend Diane when we were on the playground at recess.

"Guess what?" I said. "Tomorrow we're going to have a surprise spelling bee."

"No way," she said. "It's Wednesday, and we only have spelling bees on Friday."

"Maybe so, but I heard Sister Mary Margaret say we are, so we are."

"Say it to who?"

"Never mind," I said, knowing she'd never believe me. "She just said it."

Even then, I was smart enough to know that telling Diane I'd heard her say it in my head was dangerous. The kids at school already didn't think much of me because I was such a "good girl," so telling them that I could hear someone think out loud wasn't a good idea and would do nothing for my already-suffering reputation.

"But don't tell anyone else, okay? It's a secret," I said.

"I won't," she promised.

By the end of recess, the entire class knew.

Sure enough, the next morning Sister Mary Margaret blew the whistle she wore around her neck and announced, "All right, students. Let's see who did their spelling homework last night. Everyone line up across the wall. We're going to have a spelling bee."

My eyes and everyone else's in the class fairly popped out of our heads. Everyone quickly exchanged glances, and some kids smirked and laughed because, little did Sister know, it was no surprise.

It was a big deal to me, however. This was perhaps the first public confirmation I'd had that my vibes were reliable. The kids jumped up and ran for the blackboard, unlike the usual dread that accompanied Sister's frequent ambushes. Because of what I'd told Diane yesterday, this time they were ready.

One by one, each student rattled off the spelling words flawlessly. After three rounds, only one kid (Robert Barcelona, who always went down anyway) missed a word. Not Teddy Alvarez, who was a terrible speller. Not Bobby Castillo, who never even got the first one right. Not even Darlene Glaubitz, who intentionally missed words just to make the boys laugh. That day we all spelled like champs.

Amazed and pleasantly surprised, Sister pushed the glasses she usually wore at the tip of her nose against her face and slowly closed the spelling book. Eyeballing us one at a time, she said, "Hmm . . . it seems as if we have a miracle happening today. You've all done very well."

My heart was pounding so hard as she spoke that I thought it would fly through my chest. Astounded that what I'd heard yesterday was correct, and moved that the kids had believed me when the word spread across the playground, I nearly burst into tears. I was always on the brink of tears because I was so sensitive. But today I desperately tried to control my emotions because I didn't want to embarrass myself. Every time I did start crying for no reason, everyone laughed at me, and I hated it. I could feel all eyes on me, and it took everything in me not to lose it.

Just as we were about to be dismissed, a girl named Debbie ruined everything by saying, "Sonia told us we were going to have a spelling bee today."

She was such a jerk. I never did like that girl.

"Excuse me?" said Sister Mary Margaret. "What did you say?"

"Sonia told us, Sister. On the playground at recess yesterday." She spoke with a sharp nod of the head, looking very smug and quite pleased with herself for tattling on me.

"Yeah," piped up the other kids, wanting to be in on the bust. Even Vickie, my best friend, ganged up with the rest. It was too painful to hear. *Those dirty rats,* I thought. *How ungrateful!*

The entire class began shouting in a chorus, enjoying letting Sister in on the secret. "Sonia told us you were going to give us a spelling bee. So we knew." I sat there, my eyes now hot with tears, gripped with fear and a feeling of total abandonment. I flashed on how Jesus must have felt when he was taken to see Pontius Pilate—total betrayal.

Furious and confused, Sister stared menacingly at me, her eyes burrowing right into the center of my chest. "Is this true, Sonia? Did you tell the students about the spelling bee?"

Terrified, I couldn't speak. I could only nod yes as the tears poured down my face.

The lunch bell rang. Sister slammed her hand onto her desk and commanded, "Everyone out! And stay in single file. Now march!" The class glanced over at me with a combination of malice and pity in their eyes as I started to fall in line.

"Not you, Sonia!" Sister shrieked. "I want to speak with you at my desk."

Everyone burst out laughing.

"Silence!" Sister boomed. "Unless, of course, you want to join her."

It became so quiet you could hear a pin drop. Shaking and crying and afraid for my life, I approached her desk, watching my classmates merrily skip off to lunch. Even Vickie didn't look at me. I'd often had fantasies of being left for dead or betrayed like this.

Sister, not happy to have been outsmarted, glowered at me. "You have some explaining to do, young lady, and it better be good."

I opened my mouth, but no words came. I was unable to find my voice. I didn't even know how to begin.

She tried again. "Did you tell the other children we were going to have a spelling bee today?"

Summoning all my courage, I managed to squeak out an almost inaudible, "Yes."

"When?"

"Yesterday."

"Yesterday?"

"Yes," I said, looking down to avoid her mean expression.

She stared at me with a laserlike intensity and asked in a quiet, yet menacing, tone, "How did you know?"

"I don't know," I answered. "I just heard you say it."

"What do you mean, you heard me say it? I did *not* tell you."

"I didn't hear you say it to me. I heard you say it in my head."

Sister was silent, furious at my answer. "What do you mean, in your head?"

"I don't know," I said. "I just sat at my desk yesterday before recess and heard you say it. Just like that. I heard you say, 'I'm going to give these kids a surprise spelling bee tomorrow.' You were thinking it, and I heard you say it."

Not knowing how to handle my revelation, she resorted to her all-too-familiar assault tactic: "Don't you ever lie to me like this again. If you do, I will give you 50 whacks with my paddle." She was referring to the well-known and well-worn 18" by 4" wooden board she kept on her desk with the words "Heat for the Seat" emblazoned in red across it. It had a picture in one corner of a crying boy bending over rubbing the seat of his pants. She raised the paddle over my head and whacked me very hard. Then she whacked me again.

Holding my hands over my head to protect myself, I scrunched down and winced, my ears ringing from the pain, wondering if I should tell her I wasn't lying.

A voice popped into my head the moment I thought this: *"Don't."*

"And be glad it was a lie," she snarled, as she whacked me again, "because if you aren't lying and what you're saying is true—that you heard me think—then Lord have mercy on your soul, young lady, because that's not right."

Now that's a concept I've never heard before, I thought, as I hunched over to protect myself from further insult and injury.

"Don't you ever, ever, *ever* talk like that again," she said. "And because you *are* lying, you will stay after school for a one-hour detention and go to confession when that's over. Now, shame on you, is all I have to say. I'm so disappointed that you, of all people, would stoop so low. Just march yourself to lunch, and never let it happen again."

Tears pouring down my cheeks, my heart doing a Mexican hat dance, and confusion distorting my view, I ran out of there so fast that I ran straight into a wall.

The entire episode threw me for a loop. I always knew that Sister Mary Margaret was a grouch, and I knew she didn't think much of any of us, but I'd managed to protect myself from her bad temper by being absolutely certain to do things the way she wanted. I was even scornfully called "teacher's pet" by the class, an unenviable position, but the safest one under the circumstances.

Now, for reasons I didn't understand, I was being treated as though I'd done something terribly wrong, and I hadn't. And worse, it was public knowledge.

Up until now, my psychic experiences were reserved for my family—extremely private, and held in highest regard by my mother, and by me as well. The idea that having a psychic thought or awareness, quietly or out loud, would be anything other than cause for great self-congratulation and personal satisfaction was inconceivable.

What did she mean, "shame" on me? She should have said, "Good job. You helped everyone win the spelling bee." How unfair.

After my initial wave of terror passed, rather than feeling ashamed and full of remorse, I became angry—furious, in fact. And defiant. She wasn't going to take away my best talent, the one that already at such a young age I was intensely proud of and had been cultivating for some time. Sister was stupid for saying those things.

I sat in the lunchroom alone, the other kids having finished and gone back to the playground. Frantically trying to sort out the entire episode before I had to go back to class stamped with Sister's version of the scarlet letter, I desperately asked God, "Why did this happen?"

Chewing on the last bite of my cold Spam-and-cheese sandwich, I suddenly heard a voice, loud and clear just like the day before, only this time it was the voice of a beautiful woman soothing my injured and traumatized sensibilities like a balm. *"Forgive her, Sonia. She doesn't understand you. Just be quiet for now. We love you."*

It was my guide, Rose—the one I'd spoken to in my heart every night since I was five . . . the one I heard in my head at night just before I went to sleep. I recognized her by the feeling that came over me, as though my shredded aura had been instantly rewoven. It was absolute love.

I was so excited at being able to hear her voice as clearly as any person's that I stopped thinking about Sister Mary Margaret. In my heart, I knew that my guide, Rose, was bigger than she was and would protect me.

This was the first time I actually heard Rose speak out loud directly to me, and not just silently in my heart. I was as startled as I had been the day before when I'd heard Sister Mary Margaret thinking to herself. I started to cry, only this time in utter relief. Just then the bell rang and I had to go back to class. I composed myself because I didn't want my face to look tear stained and blotchy.

"Thank you, Rose," I said. I knew I'd be okay.

In class, Sister acted calm and neutral toward me, and I no longer felt threatened. Little did I know that she'd had just as disturbing a lunch hour as I had because she'd been forced to think about what I'd said and started to wonder about other things, too.

I didn't realize it at that very moment, but in the past 24 hours I'd discovered my *clairaudient channel*. It was to become my main psychic artery for doing my life's work. I had unknowingly opened my telepathic circuit, giving me the ability to hear my guides and psychically tune in to other people on an even deeper level than before. I'd eventually use this channel in my work as both a psychic teacher and healer. It was to become my psychic switchboard, simultaneously allowing me to tune in to others, tune in to my guides, and eventually into the matrix of the soul. At the time, however, all it meant to me was: *Thank goodness I can hear you, whoever you are, because I need help down here.*

My reality and perspective changed deeply that morning. I'd never been challenged by anyone about listening to my inner voice, nor had anyone suggested that it was a *bad* thing to do. I withstood the challenge and became more fiercely committed than ever to listening to my vibes, realizing that what I knew was important . . . and that I'd have to defend my position when I was tested.

(From *Diary of a Psychic,* Hay House, 2003)

Dr. John F. Demartini

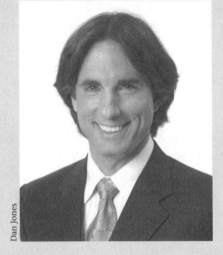

Dan Jones

Dr. John F. Demartini, the author of *The Breakthrough Experience* and *Count Your Blessings,* among other works, is a professional speaker, author, and business consultant whose clients range from Wall Street financiers, financial planners, and corporate executives to health-care professionals, actors, and sports personalities. The founder of The Concourse of Wisdom School, John began his career as a doctor of chiropractic and went on to explore more than 200 different disciplines in pursuit of what he calls Universal Principles of Life and Health. As an international speaker, he breathes new life into audiences all over the world with his enlightening perspectives, humorous observations of human nature, and practical action steps.

Website: **www.DrDemartini.com**

THEY CAN'T
TAKE AWAY YOUR
LOVE AND WISDOM

One of my most significant hidden blessings came to me in the first grade. I was a left-handed dyslexic, unable to read or comprehend, and my teacher knew little about learning disabilities. I started in the general class, was moved to a remedial reading class, and finally ended up in the "dunce class," where I sometimes had to sit in a corner and wear a conical dunce cap on my head. I felt ashamed, different, and rejected.

One day my teacher asked my parents to come to class. In front of me, she told them, "Mr. and Mrs. Demartini, your son has a learning disability. I'm afraid he will never read, write, or communicate normally. I wouldn't expect him to do much in life, and I don't think he'll go very far. If I were you, I would put him into sports." Although I didn't fully understand the significance of her words, I sensed my parents' uncertainty and concern.

I went into sports and eventually developed a real love for surfing. At the age of 14, I told my father, "I'm going to California to go surfing, Dad."

He looked me in the eye and sensed that I was sincere, and that no matter what he said, I was going to do it, because that was where I belonged. He asked me, "Are you capable of handling whatever happens? Are you willing to take whatever responsibilities come along?"

"Yes, I am."

He said, "I'm not going to fight you, son. You have my blessings."

And he prepared a notarized letter saying, "My son is not a runaway. He's not a vagrant. He's a boy with a dream."

Years later, I found out that when my dad came back from World War II, he had hoped to go to California, but didn't. When he heard me say I was going there, I believe his old dream came back to him and he thought, *I never made it, but I'm not going to stop you.*

So at the age of 14, I dropped out of school. My mom and dad gave me a ride to the freeway, lovingly said good-bye, and told me, "Go follow your dreams."

I set off hitchhiking toward California and soon arrived in El Paso, Texas. I was walking through town on my way to the West Coast, moving down a sidewalk with no place to go but straight ahead, when I saw three cowboys ahead of me.

Back in the '60s, cowboys and surfers didn't get along. An underlying war existed between the shorthaired rednecks and longhaired "white-necks." As I walked down that sidewalk with my backpack, surfboard, long hair, and headband, I knew I was about to be confronted. As I approached, they lined up across the sidewalk and stood there with their thumbs in their belts. They weren't going to let me through.

I was thinking, *Oh, God, what am I gonna do?* when all of a sudden, for the very first time, my inner voice spoke to me. It told me to . . . bark! Now, that may not have been the most inspired inner voice, but it was the only one I had. It said to bark, so I just went along with it and started to bark, "Ruff! Ruff! Raaarrrruff!" and lo and behold, the cowboys got out of my way.

For the first time, I learned that if I trusted my intuition, amazing things would happen.

I growled my way through the three men, still going, "Raaarrufff! Ruff! Ruff! RRRRUUUFFF!" and they moved out of the way, probably thinking, *This kid is nuts!* As I walked safely past the three cowboys, I felt like I had just come out of a trance. I slowly turned away from them as I came up to the corner, and there, leaning on a lamppost, roaring with laughter, was a baldheaded old bum in his 60s or so with about four days' worth of stubble. He was laughing so hard he had to hang on to the lamppost to hold himself up.

"Sonny," he said, "that's the funniest dang thing I've ever seen. You took care of them cowpokes like a pro!" He put his hand on my shoulder and walked me down the street.

He said, "Can I buy you a cup of coffee?"

I said, "No, sir, I don't drink coffee."

"Well, can I buy you a Coke?"

"Well, yes, sir!"

We walked up to a little malt shop with swivel stools along the counter. Inside, we sat down and he said, "So where you headed, sonny?"

"I'm going to California."

"Are you a runaway?"

"No, my parents gave me a ride to the freeway."

"You dropped out of school?"

"Well, yeah. I was told I would never read, write, or communicate, so I just went into sports. I'm going to California to be a surfer."

He said, "Are you finished with your Coke?"

"Yep."

"You follow me, young boy."

So I followed this scruffy man, and he took me a few blocks down the street, and then a few blocks more, and he led me through the front doors of the downtown El Paso library.

He pointed to a spot on the floor. "Put your stuff down here; it'll be safe," and we walked through the library, where he sat me down at a table.

"Sit down, young boy. Sit down and I'll be right back," and off he went into the bookshelves.

In a few minutes, he came back with a couple of books and sat down next to me. "There are two things I want to teach you, young man, two things I don't want you to ever forget. You promise?"

"Yes, sir, I do."

My newfound mentor said, "Number one, young fella, is never judge a book by its cover."

"Yes, sir."

"Because you probably think I'm a bum. But let me tell you a little secret. I'm one of the wealthiest men in America. I come from the Northeast, and I have every single thing that money has ever been able to buy—the cars, the planes, the houses. A year ago, someone very dear to me passed away, and when she went, I reflected on my life and thought, *I have everything except one experience. What's it like to have nothing and to live on the streets?* So I made a commitment to travel around America and go from city to city, with nothing, just to have that experience before I died. So, son, don't you ever judge a book by its cover, because it will fool you."

Then he grabbed my right hand and pulled it forward and set it on top of the two books he'd put there. They were the works of Aristotle and Plato, and he said with such intensity and clarity that I've never forgotten it: "You learn how to read, boy. You learn how to read, 'cause there's only two things that the world can't take away from you: your love and your wisdom. They can take away your loved ones, they can take away your money, they can take away just about everything, but they can't take away your love and wisdom. You remember that, boy."

I said, "Yes, sir, I will."

And then he walked me over a few blocks and sent me on my way to California. To this day I've never forgotten his message, and it has become the core of my belief system: *Love and wisdom are the essence of life.*

(From *The Breakthrough Experience,* Hay House, 2002)

Dr. Wayne W. Dyer

Greg Bertolini

Dr. Wayne W. Dyer is an internationally renowned author and speaker in the field of self-development. He's the author of 30 books, has created many audio programs and videos, and has appeared on thousands of television and radio shows. His books *Manifest Your Destiny, Wisdom of the Ages, There's a Spiritual Solution to Every Problem,* and *The New York Times* bestsellers *10 Secrets for Success and Inner Peace, The Power of Intention,* and *Inspiration* have all been featured as National Public Television specials.

Wayne holds a doctorate in educational counseling from Wayne State University and was an associate professor at St. John's University in New York.

Website: **www.DrWayneDyer.com**

THE MIRACLE OF
THE BUTTERFLY

The same day that I completed Chapter 17 of my book *Inspira-tion* and read it over the telephone to my editor, Joanna, on Bainbridge Island, Washington, I had the most profoundly mystical experience of being in-Spirit in all of my 65 years. (The photograph on the opposite page is a re-creation of what happened.)

When I finished up with Joanna that day, I went for my daily hour-long walk along the beach . . . but for some reason I elected to take a slightly different route along a grassy area *adjacent* to the beach. I was recalling my friend Jack Boland, a Unity minister in Detroit, who had crossed over about a decade ago. Jack loved monarch butterflies, often telling stories of how he marveled at these paper-thin creatures who migrated thousands of miles in high winds and returned to the same branch on the same tree where they first emerged from their cocoons.

Before Jack passed away, I presented him with a beautiful paperweight containing a dead monarch that I'd found in perfect condition. When he died, his wife returned it to me, telling me how much Jack loved that gift and how much he admired these amazing creatures who had such mysterious intelligence built into their brains, which are the size of a pinhead.

Jack always told me to "be in a state of gratitude," and he ended every sermon with this message to God: "Thank You, thank You, thank You." On three occasions since his death, a monarch butter-fly has landed on my body. Since these creatures studiously avoid human contact, each time this has happened I've thought about Jack and said to myself, *Thank You, God—thank You, thank You.*

Anyway, as I walked, feeling grateful for having completed the second-to-last chapter of my book, a monarch landed on the ground, three feet in front of me. I said Jack's magic words to myself *(thank You, God—thank You, thank You)*, and felt deep appreciation for my life and the beauty of the day. The butterfly stayed right there until I approached, then he flapped his wings several times and flew away. Thinking of Jack and feeling a little bewildered and immensely thankful, I watched this creature in flight, now 40 or 50 yards away.

As God is my witness, the butterfly made a U-turn and not only headed in my direction, but landed right smack on my finger! Needless to say, I was shocked—but not totally surprised. I must confess that it seems to me that the more I stay in-Spirit, the more I experience synchronicities similar to this one. But what followed did border on the incredible, even for me.

This little creature became my constant companion for the next two and a half hours—he sat first on one hand and then moved to my other hand, never even coming close to flying away. He seemed to be trying to communicate with me by moving his wings back and forth, and even opening and closing his tiny mouth as if attempting to speak . . . and as crazy as it may sound, I felt a deep affinity for this precious living being. I sat on the ground and simply stayed with my new fragile friend for 30 or so minutes. Then I called Joanna from my cell phone, and she was also stunned by the synchronicity, insisting that I somehow get a picture of this event.

At this point I decided to return to my home, approximately a mile from where I was sitting, with my new companion. I returned along the beach walk, where the winds were brisk—the butterfly's wings were pushed by these high gusts, but he clung to my finger, and even moved to my other hand without making any effort to leave. As I walked, I encountered a four-year-old girl with her mother. The girl was sobbing over some perceived tragedy in her young life, and when I showed her my "pet" butterfly, her expression went from sad to blissful in one split second. She smiled from ear to ear and asked me all about the winged creature on my forefinger.

When I got home, I walked upstairs as I was talking on my cell phone to my friend Reid Tracy (the president of Hay House). He laughed with me as I related the bizarre synchronicity at play in this very moment. I said, "Reid, it's been 90 minutes, and this little guy has adopted me." Reid also encouraged me to get a photograph, since this experience was obviously in complete harmony with what I was writing.

I left my new friend—whom I was now calling "Jack"—sitting on the handwritten Chapter 17 on my lanai, and went downstairs. I found Cindy, a young woman who works nearby, and asked her to run to the store and purchase a disposable camera. She did, and I went back to the patio, put my hand next to Jack, and watched him jump right onto my finger! It appeared that my butterfly companion had decided that he was now going to live with me forever.

After another hour or so of meditating and communing with this little creature of God—and pondering this event as the most unprecedented and out-of-the-ordinary spiritual episode I'd ever encountered—I gently placed Jack back on my manuscript while I proceeded to take a long, hot shower. When I returned to the patio, I placed my finger near my winged friend as I'd done many times in the previous 150 minutes, but he now seemed like a totally different little critter. He fluttered away, landed on a table, flapped his wings twice, and flew off, straight up toward the heavens. Moments with him were now history, but I still had the photographs, which I treasure.

The next morning, I decided to watch one of my favorite films, *Brother Sun, Sister Moon*, which I hadn't viewed for more than a decade. And sure enough—in the opening scenes of Franco Zeffirelli's interpretation of the life of St. Francis, there he was . . . with a butterfly alighting on his fingers.

(From *Inspiration*, Hay House, 2006)

John Edward

Devon Cass

John Edward is an internationally acclaimed psychic medium, and author of the *New York Times* bestsellers *One Last Time, Crossing Over,* and *Final Beginnings,* among other works. In addition to hosting his own syndicated television show, *Crossing Over with John Edward,* John has been a frequent guest on *Larry King Live* and many other talk shows, and was featured in the HBO documentary *Life After Life.* He publishes his own newsletter and also conducts workshops and seminars around the country. John lives in New York with his family.

Website: **www.johnedward.net**

A SPIRITUAL
MAIL CARRIER

It was February 2003, and I was in Houston giving a seminar, which I started in my usual way—giving a talk about how the process of getting information from the Other Side works and taking questions from the audience. Some people asked the standard questions about my personal experiences, while others took the microphone to thank me for doing what I do. One woman in particular almost reduced me to tears when she shared that she'd recently lost a baby, and watching my TV show *Crossing Over* had become a form of therapy for her in dealing with her overwhelming grief.

As soon as the lecture and Q&A period were over, I was pulled to the middle section of the room. I remember standing on the stage of the theater, extending my arm out in front of me and pointing—drawing a straight line from me to the center of the audience. As I did so, I had a powerful image in my mind's eye . . . it was the space shuttle *Columbia*. I just knew . . . I *knew* . . . this message coming through had something to do with the explosion that had occurred just three weeks earlier, and someone right in front of me was connected to it.

محм

My own connection to this disaster began before it even happened. I'd watched the shuttle take off on television on January

16 from home with my wife, Sandra, and I remember getting a really bad feeling as it shot into the sky. It was just a general "not good" feeling—nothing specific. That's how I often feel these kinds of premonitions—my guides don't show me any details. So when people ask why I don't do anything to prevent some tragedy, that's my answer: I don't know myself what's going to happen.

Five days later in Los Angeles, en route to Australia, I did a magazine interview, and the reporter asked me if I get premonitions, and could I give her my most recent one. I said sure, but it wasn't a very positive one. I told her that I'd watched the *Columbia* launch and felt concern for the astronauts. The reporter immediately jumped on it and asked, "Is it going to crash? Or explode?" and I freaked out a bit, realizing maybe I'd said too much. I tried to backpedal a bit to calm us both down, saying, "No, no . . . I just don't have a good feeling."

That was the last I thought about the shuttle until the night of January 29, 2003, when I was having dinner in Melbourne, Australia, with all the people who had helped organize the tour. My friend Natasha Stoynoff, a *People* magazine correspondent, and I were digging into our steaks and making idle chitchat about the local wine when I froze in midsentence, my fork hanging from my fingers.

"John . . . what's wrong?" Natasha asked. She recognized that *look* on my face.

"I feel like something is exploding," I told her, putting my fork down—"and there's some kind of . . . Israeli connection to it."

What? When? *Where?* She asked about a dozen reporter-like questions, whipping out her pen and notebook, but I couldn't answer any of them because I didn't know the answers myself. I told her not to worry about it for now, and I pushed the feeling out of my mind. I kind of thought, *Okay . . . Israel . . . they have explosions there all the time . . . this isn't so psychic of me.* We both went to sleep that night feeling a little uneasy.

The next day we boarded the plane for the long flight back home. As we waited for our connecting flight in Los Angeles, there it was on CNN: The shuttle had exploded that morning, killing its entire seven-member crew—including the first Israeli in history to ever make that expedition. Sitting there in the airport, I felt the deep sadness I always experience when a bad premonition comes true, and I said a silent prayer for the crew members and their families.

"I feel really awkward saying this," I told the audience in Houston, "but is there someone here connected with someone who perished in the recent shuttle disaster?"

There was an immediate hush over the room. I felt uncomfortable asking this question because the time frame was so close to the event, and I was sure that anyone connected would still be emotionally raw. I always tell people that mediumship is not a cure for grief, and can only be helpful at the right time during a person's journey *through* this grief—which is rarely right after their loved one has passed.

I was hesitant to bring up the shuttle disaster for fear that the loss was too recent, but my main rule in this work is: *If they* [my guides] *show it, so do I.* A big part of the process is not editing what I get.

"Someone right in that section," I said, pointing out front, "is connected with one of the astronauts who crossed on the space shuttle *Columbia* three weeks ago." A woman directly in front of me, in the very back of the room, stood up.

"My husband is Rick Husband's cousin," she said.

I didn't know whom she was talking about, since I didn't know the names of the astronauts. The woman explained that Rick Husband was the commander of the *Columbia,* and a cousin by marriage. Once she validated this, the information started to flow. Rick said that there would be additional information about the disaster that the families of the astronauts would be receiving—perhaps a video, which may or may not become public knowledge. There were also "audible" messages of the shuttle crew on tape that the public didn't know about yet, but would soon. I was shown that the passing of the astronauts was fast and somewhat of a surprise, and they were unconscious before anything happened to their physical bodies.

"It's as if they were asleep," I told the audience, as I dropped my head to the side in a sleeping position to show what I was feeling and seeing. Everyone applauded at that, in relief for the astronauts and their families.

"Rick comes from a religious family . . ." was the next bit of information I got. The entire room nodded in unison. Everyone seemed to know this about their hometown son except me.

"There's an 'LN' name . . . like Lynne . . . connected to Rick. Is this you?"

She shook her head no. And then I felt a split pull—as if I were a sheet of paper torn in half and separated in two opposite directions.

"Is there someone else here in the room who also knows Rick? Or is there someone else here connected to *another* member of the shuttle crew?"

A petite woman about ten rows in front of me raised her hand. "Yes," she said, "I knew the Israeli astronaut on that flight. His name was Ilan [pronounced *Ee-LAN*]."

Okay, so that explained the "Lynne" name. For me, when I hear names that start with a vowel, I will not hear that first vowel. I'll hear the consonant sounds following the vowel as strong and pre-dominant. So in this case, "Ilan" became more of a "Lan" or "Lin" sound in my head, because I didn't hear the "E" sound. Information started coming through from this second astronaut.

"He wants me to acknowledge his kids . . . and something about the music. Was someone singing either to him from here, or was he singing to here from there?"

"He and his wife had a song about being far away," the woman answered in an emotional whisper, "and she sang it to him while he was there." At this point, I was getting emotional, too.

"And his daughter, his little girl," the woman continued, "watched her father take off in the shuttle. And at that moment, she said out loud, 'I just lost my daddy.'"

All right, now I was doing everything possible to keep myself from losing it right there onstage. Normally when I do readings, I can stay detached from the feeling part of it—that's how I'm able to relay such poignant details time after time without becoming a sobbing wreck. But this last image of the astronaut's little girl waving bye-bye to her daddy just got me. Ever since my son, Justin, was born, readings that deal with parent-child relationships have had an even deeper and more heartbreaking effect on me than ever before.

After the event, my assistant, Carol, told me that it was highly publicized and reported in the newspapers that the astronaut's daughter had said those words as the shuttle blasted off. So did the little girl sense what was going to happen? Well, I do believe our soul decides when it's completed its lessons here in the physical world. And when that time comes, we allow ourselves to exit. Some events, which we call "accidents," may not be accidents at all in terms of the Other Side.

By the end of those two readings in Houston, the astronauts had also brought through the parents of the two women. I hope that they found comfort in that, and in knowing that the astronauts saw them as an opportunity to pass on messages to their loved ones here and let them know they're okay.

Two weeks after the seminar, on March 1, news reports validated the information that came through in the reading. The New York *Daily News* revealed that a video had been found in Texas showing the crew's last moments—laughing, talking, and not knowing anything was wrong. It was "a remarkable fragment of video that survived the terrible fires that consumed the space shuttle *Columbia*," the report said. "There is not even a hint of concern, anxiety—nothing . . . trauma specialists said the cheerful images would bring comfort to the families, who were shown the video and agreed it should be made public."

A month after my stay in Houston, I was contacted by Nancy Marlowe Sheppard, Rick Husband's relative whom I'd read for at the seminar. Sheppard, a retired schoolteacher, was eager to tell me what had happened to her before she even got to the reading that day. Ever since the shuttle explosion, she'd been having strong feelings that she needed to attend a taping of *Crossing Over*—that if she did, something important might happen. When she learned about the seminar that was to happen nearby, she called the venue to get a ticket but was told it had been sold out for months.

Nancy recalled, "I said to the woman on the phone, 'Look, I *really* need to go. Can't you try again?'"

Often, I believe, the Other Side really does have a hand in getting people where they need to be. In many cases, people who tried to get tickets for *Crossing Over*, or for a seminar or private sitting, often got them as a fluke or seemingly by "coincidence"—and they ended up having a dramatic reading.

But, once again, I don't believe anything is ever a coincidence—the ticket agent suddenly "found" two tickets for Nancy to the sold-out seminar. As she was preparing to leave her house for the event, she had hopes that her deceased parents might come through that day. But before she left home, Nancy had what can only be described as a premonition: Rick's energy came through to her. "I felt Rick's presence," she said, "and I knew he was going to come through at the reading." Her premonition included information that "he and the rest of the crew did not suffer and were grateful for the love America had shown to them."

The message surprised Nancy—but it wasn't a complete shock. "I've always been intuitive," says Nancy, "ever since I was a child. But I always pushed away the hunches, the feelings, the visions, the knowing."

It's not uncommon for many people to feel in touch with the spiritual world—whether they get a thought, hear a voice, or smell a whiff of perfume that Mom used to wear—most people at one time or another have had psychic experiences. We all have this ability within us to different degrees, but rather than pay attention to it, many ignore it. Nancy had tried to ignore her "hunches" her entire life, but on the day of the reading, she couldn't do it anymore.

"I was sitting in the second-to-last row, in the last seat. I know you couldn't even see me from up on the stage," recalled Nancy. "When you asked if there was anyone related to the *Columbia* crew and I stood up, I was the only one standing in the room, and my heart was beating so fast. I told you I was connected to Rick, and then you said, 'Rick Husband is *here.*' One of the messages you got was that Rick was a religious man—and it's true. He went to church, spoke in Sunday school, and did all sorts of things like that," she said. "And then my parents came through in the reading. . . ."

Nancy was overjoyed that her mom and dad came through and made a "cameo appearance," giving accurate family birthdays, anniversaries, and illnesses so that she knew it was them. But what affected her most was something I said to the group at the end of the evening.

Nancy remembered, "You paused, and then you said, 'Did someone here know *before* the seminar that this was going to happen?' That's the part that was so awesome for me. I was still standing, and I said, 'I knew!'"

A month after the seminar, Nancy sent a letter to Rick's mother and wife to tell them about her experience, hoping that the words would give them peace. That day in Houston was Nancy's introduction to being a "spiritual mail carrier." It began with her premonition earlier in the day and continued with her delivering a message for the Other Side when she mailed that letter to Rick's family.

Being a spiritual mail carrier is a job many of us undertake although we may not be aware of it. The young girl watching her father leave on the shuttle was passing along a message, too. You don't need to be a medium to work with the Other Side; you just need to be open to the vibrations and be willing to listen.

"I really think I was supposed to be there," Nancy reflected. "I think that's why I got the ticket at the last minute. I think Rick Husband knew I'd be there and chose me to get his message out."

(From *After Life,* Princess Books/Hay House, 2003)

Lesley Garner

Romas Foord

Lesley Garner, the author of *Everything I've Ever Done That Worked,* has been taking notes all her life. Her thoughts and observations have been published as magazine features, profiles, and newspaper columns for publications such as the *London Daily Telegraph, Daily Mail,* and *Evening Standard* in the UK. She has been an art critic, a book and film reviewer, and when she's not writing, she loves to get out and sing great choral music. She has traveled widely, has lived in Ethiopia and Afghanistan, and currently lives in London.

BEING HUMAN

Sometimes people lose everything. The crisis that comes into their lives isn't one of the heart, the ego, or the bank balance. They haven't lost a job, a lover, or even a limb. Their view of their future hasn't simply vanished as a castle in the air quivers and melts in the mind; it has crumbled into real dust before their physical eyes. A familiar wall hides a sniper. A beloved home explodes in flames. The men who support you are killed or have vanished. The women you love and honor are raped. The children starve. The country lies in ruins. What, in these extremes of human experience, works?

One hot May day in 1999, I walked on a Macedonian hillside among people who were barely living a human existence. The hillside had been bulldozed bare of all vegetation, even grass. The green hills of the Balkans were all around, but wire fences marked out blinding acres of rough stones. I was in Cigrane, the latest refugee camp created in Macedonia for the thousands of refugees fleeing across the borders from Kosovo. It was for Albanian Kosovars who had abandoned their homes to Serbian militia and who had spent days and weeks trekking through the mountains to a place of safety.

Cigrane wasn't a place where anyone wanted to be. It was so new and raw that tents were still being erected, and families were sleeping out on uncushioned stones on the bare mountainside. Outside the camp gates waited red buses crammed with exhausted people who had lined up to walk across the Macedonian border. I'd seen the buses earlier waiting at the border post; and the shocked, drained, and exhausted faces of the people in them were like no human faces I'd ever seen before. They were the faces of those who had surrendered, the unfocused, burned-out visages of people at the edge of endurance. When I saw them, I thought I knew what the Jews looked like on the trains that took them to the concentration camps.

Five thousand people a day were coming into Cigrane. While the newest group of refugees waited passively in the buses, inside the gates I walked about and talked to the people who had already been there a night. A system was beginning to establish itself: Where tents had been erected and blankets distributed, the human urge to create a home was asserting itself.

People had no more than the clothes they'd been wearing when they fled the Serbs. To have clean clothes, they had to lie naked under their blankets while their clothes dried on the ropes of their tent. Mothers with babies lined up in the hot May sun for the daily ration of three disposable diapers. Further down the hillside, a truck unloaded the sole food allowance of one roll of bread a day. There was another line at a table set up by the Red Cross to register people looking for lost relatives.

Everywhere I walked I could feel a palpable atmosphere of bewilderment, fatigue, and frustration. These were the surface emotions stirred up by the chaos of the camp. Beneath the minute-by-minute anxiety of trying to function in this raw, hostile environment, each individual was holding deeper feelings of loss, grief, and a terrible fear of what the future might bring.

And yet in the most difficult circumstances, the human spirit irresistibly asserts itself. Children were playing and laughing by the water pipes. Little twig brooms already stood outside the doors of the tents as a witness to the effort to create order out of overwhelming disorder.

I'll never forget standing on the most exposed area of the camp, a white slope of sharp stones scattered with the belongings of the small groups of people who'd spent the night on the open mountainside. I was talking to a weary middle-aged couple about their sleepless night when a striking little group came straggling up the hillside toward us. Like Mother Courage, Begishe, a 32-year-old woman, grubby but spirited, was leading her ragtag band of five children up the hill. They were dusty-faced, weary, their arms full of bags and blankets and babies. They'd been sleeping under the stars and on the stones of Cigrane for five days. Before that, Begishe had led them through the mountains from village to village, ever since the Serbian militia had attacked their village and driven them up into makeshift shelters in the forest. Their father was in Germany, but the dusty little family radiated a tough spirit of survival and resilience.

As they stood talking to the older couple, I expressed my inadequate sympathy for their situation, and it was my awkward words of kindness rather than their hardship that brought tears to their eyes. I wanted to know what it was that gave them the spirit and courage to keep going in these extreme and chaotic circumstances. It was the older woman who told me, "We do everything together. We give each other moral support. We are very human to each other."

It was a very striking and humbling lesson. When everything intangible has gone—status, worldly identity, optimism for the future, ambition—people can still be human to each other. When everything tangible has gone—home, land, family, farm animals, clothes, and possessions—people can still be human to each other. Being human is all they have left.

What did this woman mean, homeless on her open mountainside, by being human? After all, the gunmen who had driven these people out of their homes and country were being human, too. I've thought often about this, and I think that being human means being vulnerable and open. It means being in empathy with other people and knowing that you're not different from them. It means being part of one organism, not safe or separate. It means abandoning roles, expectations, judgments, and opposition. It means losing the need to control other people. It means being responsive to your environment and not shut off from it, let alone seized by the need to exploit and destroy it. It means reaching out rather than shutting off. It certainly *doesn't* mean discriminating, oppressing, excluding, and even killing.

Good fortune and bad fortune can both encourage a sense of humanity. Good fortune does it by making us relaxed, trusting, and unafraid; bad fortune by making us recognize our irreducible human nature and our interdependency with others. But good fortune carries the danger of complacency and detachment from other people's experiences. The enclaves of the rich aren't famous for their humanity, no matter how many checks the rich may sign for the poor. It's ironic that the great qualities of openness, generosity, and kindness often only surface in extreme circumstances—the London Blitz, or September 11 in the U.S. In circumstances of overwhelming threat, when everything familiar has gone, being human is all that works.

I once heard Ram Dass say that the challenge of life is to keep your heart open in hell. These were striking words, but when I remember those Kosovars in the stones and dust, I wonder if it isn't easier to keep your heart open in hell when your heart is all that's left. The challenge is to stay human when the complexity of daily life returns, along with the suffocation of possessions and the seeking and maintaining of status.

I know one truth: As sure as the sun rises, life will get difficult again, which is why I'm writing these things down. It is my sincere hope that they'll help in the magnificent but sometimes overwhelming business of *being human*.

(From *Everything I've Ever Done That Worked,* Hay House, 2005)

Keith D. Harrell

Rick Diamond

Keith D. Harrell is a dynamic life coach and motivational speaker and the author of *An Attitude of Gratitude* and *Attitude Is Everything for Success.* As president of Harrell Performance Systems, Keith has created a firm specializing in helping those in the corporate marketplace achieve and maintain their goals through the power of a positive attitude. In August 2000, Keith was inducted into the NSA Speaker Hall of Fame, an honor given for a lifetime of speaking excellence and professionalism; and one of the country's leading lecture agencies has put him on its list of "22 Guaranteed Standing Ovations."

Website: **www.keithharrell.com**

Whatever It
Takes to Succeed

I had wanted to play pro basketball for as long as I could remember, but on the day of the NBA draft in my last year of college basketball eligibility, that dream came to an end. However, I didn't let that setback stop me from pursuing success. I set up a new game plan: Instead of the NBA, I chose IBM.

⌒

I called up my cousin Kenny Lombard and said, "Kenny, I'm ready to play another game."

"What are you talking about?" he asked.

"Basketball's been good to me, but I want to play the business game. I want to be successful, and I think that what basketball did for me then, business can do for me now. I think I'd like to work for the company you work for. Who are they again?"

"IBM," he replied.

"Do you think I have what it takes?"

My cousin was quiet for a moment, then he responded, "Keith, I believe you've got what it takes, but it's going to take even more effort than you put in at the gym to become a great business player. . . ."

Kenny kept talking, and I loved what I was hearing, because in my mind he was creating a parallel between business and sports: If you work hard at it, you'll succeed . . . as long as you don't allow fear or doubt to get in the way.

As fate would have it, IBM wasn't hiring at the time that Kenny and I had this conversation, but he said, "Just because they're not hiring *now* doesn't mean that we can't start the preparation."

"All right, I'm ready," I responded with enthusiasm. "Let's go for it!"

My success had always been a result of people coaching me, and I understood the value of mentors. Kenny was just a couple years older than I, but he was way ahead of me on the business scene. He'd come to IBM as a sales representative and had already been promoted to a position in marketing. I was thrilled that he was willing to sign on as my mentor to help me get hired there. Just as I'd spent many hours in the gym warming up for a big game, I was ready to spend just as many hours in a study setting, preparing for my job interview.

"I'll give you every Saturday morning," Kenny graciously volunteered. "We'll practice interview skills, and you'll learn the company jargon and brush up on basic business issues. But listen to me, Keith: Since you're taking up my time, I'm going to hold you accountable for the work I want you to do before each of our meetings."

"Okay," I agreed, eager to do whatever was necessary to succeed in my new endeavor.

"I'm going to give you information to study, books to read, and problems to work on," he continued.

"I'll do it," I said.

"And one more thing," he added. "When we meet, I expect you to show up on time."

"I will."

"If you don't meet these criteria, I'll get in your face. Do you understand?"

I said I did.

Preparation for the first Saturday-morning meeting began days ahead of time when I received a phone call from Kenny. "I just wanted to remind you that you have an appointment with me this Saturday," he said.

"I know," I replied. "I'm looking forward to it."

"The appointment is at 8 A.M.," Kenny continued, "and here's what I want you to know. We're going to imagine that this is a *real interview* at IBM. I want you to pretend that you don't know me. So bring your résumé; park in front of my house; knock on the door; introduce yourself, and say that you have an 8 A.M. interview with Ken Lombard, the sales manager. Then we'll begin the interview."

"Great," I said, getting more excited as he spoke.

I tried my best to get ready for the "interview" all week. On Friday night, a couple of buddies called to see if I wanted to play basketball the next morning. "I won't be playing any Saturday-morning basketball for a while," I informed them.

"Why?" they asked.

"I'm practicing so that I can get a job at IBM."

They snickered and said, "Tell us, Keith, how long do you have to 'practice' before they'll give you a job?"

Imagine their response when I admitted, "Well, they're not even hiring right now."

The laughter on the other end of the line was uproarious. "That's a good one."

"Yeah, well, listen up," I asserted. "I'm getting ready so that when they *do* begin hiring, I'll get the job."

At a few minutes before eight on Saturday morning, I pulled my car up to Kenny's house. I walked to the front door, knocked, and was greeted very formally by my cousin.

"Yes?" he said, acting as if he didn't know me.

"My name is Keith Harrell," I began. "I have an eight o'clock appointment with Ken Lombard."

"Please, come in and sit down," Kenny said as he led me into his office.

I followed him in, sat down, and was sure everything was off to a good start, when suddenly Kenny stopped pretending and looked straight into my eyes.

"The interview is over!" he announced.

"Why?" I asked in disbelief.

"Look at the way you're dressed," he answered, pointing at my clothes.

I looked down at my outfit and thought, *I look pretty cool*. I was wearing blue suede shoes, a blue silk shirt with an open collar, and a gold chain around my neck. I was confused. "What's wrong with the way I'm dressed?"

"You look as if you're planning on steppin' out," Kenny said. "As if you're going to the disco, not IBM."

"So what should I wear?"

"That's your assignment for next week." He smiled. "Two things: First, go out and buy a copy of the book called *Dress for Success,* by John T. Molloy, and read it. Second, on Monday morning I want you to go downtown and stand in front of the IBM building. See what the employees are wearing. That's how I want you to present yourself. So when you come back next Saturday, dress appropriately, and we'll continue. If you're not dressed right, I'll send you home again."

I couldn't believe it. "That's it for today?"

"Yes," Kenny replied. "It's over. Do you know why?"

"Why?"

"Because you *flunked*." With that, he got up and showed me to the door.

Naturally, I went right out and bought *Dress for Success* and devoured it. Then I made sure I was downtown early Monday morning as the IBM executives headed into their offices. And when I met with Kenny the next weekend, I didn't get sent home.

The Saturday sessions lasted for several months. Kenny did a wonderful job of coaching me, leaving no stone unturned. For example, he helped me a great deal with my diction—teaching me to talk like a business person and to lose the slang that was second nature when I spoke with family and friends. When I hung out with them, everything was "Yeah, man," or "Ya know."

"There's a difference between how you talk to an IBM customer and how you talk to your buddies when you're playing basketball," he told me.

I learned new business vocabulary and appropriate etiquette; as well as posture, presentation, and poise. It was as if I were working toward my MBA every Saturday morning. Plus, I learned more and more about the inner workings of IBM. I knew how sales were going in the Seattle office compared to other offices in the region, I could name the local managers and cite their successes during the prior year, and I gained a solid understanding of the structure of the company.

During this time in IBM's history, the company's workforce was divided into three different divisions: The Data Processing Division sold mainframe computers; the General Systems Division sold midrange computers; and the Office Products Division (always referred to as OPD by IBM employees) sold copiers, typewriters, word-processing equipment, and other office-related products. Inside IBM, this last division was considered the "lowest" of the three. I became very familiar with OPD because I was researching it on a weekly basis.

But besides turning me into a walking IBM encyclopedia, Kenny also helped me take an objective look at my strengths and weaknesses. He showed me how to counter any of my weaknesses by focusing on a strength. "I notice from looking over your résumé," he said, as if he were a manager interviewing me, "that you don't have a business degree. I also see that you haven't taken any computer or business courses."

I was ready with an answer. "Sir, my father teaches business classes at the college level, so I assure you, I know the importance of a balance sheet and an income statement, as well as assets and liabilities."

Kenny hesitated, "Yes, but—"

"Sir, if I may continue," I pressed on. "Notice what I *do* have. I have leadership qualities that will lend themselves well to this position. I played varsity basketball at Seattle University for four years. And for three of those years I was the team captain."

"That's good," Kenny answered.

"I know the importance of learning about the competition. For example, I know that our competitors are Xerox, Wang, Lanier, and Kodak, to name a few. I know how important it is to learn about their offense and their defense so we can be victorious over them."

Kenny smiled. "Tell me more."

"The experience of being a team captain also taught me how to take charge. And I know that as a salesman, it's important for me to take charge of my customers and my territory and to make my quota. I want to do all I can to move the business forward."

Kenny was pleased with my response. "You've done a great job answering my questions. You've applied your strengths as a way of offsetting your weaknesses. I think it's time to set up a mock interview with somebody from IBM."

"That's great!" I exclaimed.

"A good friend of mine is the assistant to the regional manager here in Seattle. I want you to call him and schedule an appointment. Take your résumé with you, and as always, pretend that this is the real thing. Are you ready for this next step?"

"I believe I am," I answered.

The day of the "pretend" interview arrived, and I went to visit Kenny's friend. I was nervous, but I knew I wanted this opportunity more than anything, so I just stayed focused and followed my game plan.

The interviewer asked me many of the same questions that Kenny and I had gone over for weeks, and it felt good to know the appropriate responses. But I also remember him asking me a question that I hadn't anticipated: "Keith, how will you stay motivated in a job like this one?"

I answered this one without any help from my cousin. "Well, it's all about *setting goals*. I'll set goals to reach my sales quota, and I'll make it my mission to get promoted to marketing manager. I'll draft a variety of objectives that are both achievable and challenging enough to push me to maximize myself in this company, and reaching them will keep me motivated."

It was a natural response; after all, setting goals had served me well in sports and in earning my degree. The assistant to the regional manager was impressed, and the entire interview was a very positive experience. When it was over, he complimented me on how prepared I was. He offered two or three pieces of advice that would strengthen my interviewing techniques, and then agreed to meet with me again in about a month for another trial run.

I became obsessed: I was going to be hired by IBM, and nothing was going to get in my way. I spent the next few weeks in constant study; as a result, the follow-up mock interview with the assistant to the regional manager went even better. In fact, it went so well that he made the following suggestion: "Keith, I think you're ready, so I'd like to set you up for a courtesy interview."

"Really?"

"Yes, but I emphasize *courtesy* because IBM is still not hiring. But we're always looking for potential talent somewhere down the line. Are you interested?"

"Absolutely—you tell me when and where and I'll be there."

An appointment was set, and I was on fire. Anybody who'd sit still long enough would get to hear my presentation for the interview. My mom heard it so many times she could quote it back to me. I made my pitch to my sister and to all my friends. I lived, ate, and slept that IBM interview.

I also stepped everything up a couple of notches with Kenny. We went from Saturday-only sessions to Saturdays plus two or three nights a week, and I went to the local library and studied in addition to that—I was as prepared as I could be. My meeting would be with Mr. Coby Sillers, an IBM manager in the sales division known for his thorough and intense style. He was tough, but I was ready.

"You didn't take any business courses in college, Keith," he began. "What makes you feel that you're qualified to work for IBM? What makes you equipped for a business like ours?"

I smiled, took a deep breath, and began. "Mr. Sillers, I spent four years in college, and I graduated on time. My major, community service, taught me how to deal with all kinds of people and how to build and manage relationships. These skills are especially important in today's market, where a successful businessperson has to cultivate partnerships, work as a member of a team, and know what it takes to win. I was a starter on my basketball team all four years in college, which proves that I'm a hard worker. I was the team captain for three of those years, which further demonstrates my leadership abilities and shows that I know about preparation and competition, and I have the right attitude. My dad's been teaching business for more than 20 years now at Seattle Community College, so I know the basics. I'm confident that I have what I need to do this job, and what I don't know, I can learn. I assure you, I can handle anything IBM asks me to do."

It appeared that the interview was going well. I was satisfied with my response, and I was delighted that I'd spent so much time in preparation for this session. Eventually, Coby Sillers got around to one of the questions that IBM considers crucial in all job interviews: "Keith, how would you sell me this pencil?" He pointed to one lying on his desk.

"Mr. Sillers, before I sell you anything, let me take the time to understand exactly what your needs are. I want to sell you what you need, not what I *think* you need. My purpose in being here is to form a relationship—a partnership. So let me ask *you* some questions so I can better understand your needs."

Mr. Sillers liked my answer. We had another few meetings together, and then the process was considered complete. I had a good feeling. I'd prayed and I'd prepared—the rest of it was out of my hands.

I set my sights high, but the rest of my family had their doubts during the training process. My sister thought I was crazy; and to my amazement, my mom, who'd always supported me in everything, thought this was a far-fetched plan. She let me know in little ways, such as bringing home job applications for employers such as Boeing and the city of Seattle. Both offered great opportunities, but my focus was on IBM.

I honestly believed that IBM was the *only* company that could meet my needs. In my opinion, they were the best company in the world because they truly respected the individual and were all about performance, excellence, and striving to be the best with the customer. They so completely coincided with my sports philosophy that I was convinced it was Big Blue or nothing.

You can imagine how happy I was the day the phone rang.

"Hello?" I answered.

"Is this Mr. Keith Harrell?"

"Yes, it is."

"Well, congratulations, Mr. Harrell. Your first day of work at IBM is October 17th."

(From *An Attitude of Gratitude,* Hay House, 2003)

Esther and Jerry Hicks

Esther and **Jerry Hicks**, the authors of *Ask and It Is Given, The Amazing Power of Deliberate Intent,* and *The Law of Attraction,* produce the leading-edge Abraham-Hicks teachings on the art of allowing our natural Well-Being to come forth. While presenting open workshops in up to 60 cities per year, the Hickses have now published more than 700 Abraham-Hicks books, cassettes, CDs, videos, and DVDs.

Their internationally acclaimed Website is: **www.abraham-hicks.com.**

She Speaks
with Spirits!

"**S**heila speaks with spirits!" our friends said. "She'll be here next week, and you can make an appointment with her and ask her anything you like!"

That's about the last thing on this earth that I would ever want to do, I thought, but at the same time I heard Jerry, my husband, saying, "We really would like to make an appointment. How do we go about doing that?"

⌒

That was 1984, and in the four years that Jerry and I had been married, we'd never had an argument or even exchanged cross words. We were two joyous people, living happily ever after with each other, and compatible on nearly every subject that came up. The only discomfort that I ever felt was when Jerry would entertain friends with one of his stories from 20 years earlier, relating his experiences with the Ouija board. If we were at a restaurant or some other public place when I sensed one of those stories coming on, I would politely (or sometimes not so politely), excuse myself and retreat to the ladies' room, sit in the bar, or take a walk to the car until I believed that sufficient time had passed and the account would be over. Happily, Jerry eventually stopped telling those stories when I was around.

I wasn't what you'd call a religious girl, but I'd attended enough Sunday-school classes to develop a very strong fear of evil and the devil. Thinking back, I'm not really sure if our Sunday-school teachers had actually devoted a greater proportion of our classes to teaching us to fear the devil or if that's simply what stood out in my mind. But that is, for the most part, what I remember from those years.

So, as I'd been taught, I carefully avoided anything that could possibly have any connection to the devil. One time when I was a young woman, I was sitting in a drive-in theater and happened to look out the back window of the car at the other movie screen and saw a horrible scene from *The Exorcist* (a movie that I'd purposely avoided seeing), and what I saw, without hearing the sound, affected me so strongly that I had nightmares for weeks.

⌒

"I'll make that appointment for you with Sheila," our friend told Jerry.

Jerry spent the next few days writing down his questions. He said he had some that he'd saved up since he was a small child. I didn't make a list. Instead, I struggled with the idea of going at all.

As we pulled into the driveway of a beautiful house in the heart of Phoenix, Arizona, I remember thinking, *What am I getting myself into?* We walked up to the front door, and a very nice woman greeted us and showed us into a lovely living room where we could wait for our scheduled appointment.

The house was large, simply but beautifully furnished, and very quiet. I remember feeling a sort of reverence, like being in a church.

Then a big door opened, and two pretty women dressed in fresh, brightly colored cotton blouses and skirts entered the room. Apparently we were the first appointment after lunch; both women looked happy and refreshed. I felt myself relax a little bit. Maybe this wasn't going to be so weird after all.

Soon we were invited into a lovely bedroom where three chairs were situated near the foot of the bed. Sheila was sitting on the edge of the bed, and her assistant sat in one of the chairs with a small tape recorder on the table beside her. Jerry and I sat in the other two chairs, and I braced myself for whatever was about to happen.

The assistant explained that Sheila was going to relax and release her consciousness, and then Theo, a nonphysical entity, would address us. When that happened, we'd be free to talk about anything we desired.

Sheila lay across the end of the bed, only a few feet from where we were seated, and breathed deeply. Soon, an unusual-sounding voice abruptly said, "It is the beginning, is it not? You have questions?"

I looked at Jerry, hoping that he was ready to start, because I knew that I was *not* ready to talk with whoever was now speaking to us. Jerry leaned forward; he was eager to ask his first question.

I relaxed as Theo's words slowly came out of Sheila's mouth. And while I knew that it was Sheila's voice we were hearing, I somehow also knew that something far different from Sheila was the source of these marvelous answers.

Jerry said he'd been saving his questions up since he was five years old, and he asked them as rapidly as he could. Our 30 minutes passed so quickly, but during that time, somehow, without my speaking a word, my fear of this strange experience lifted, and I was filled with a feeling of well-being that surpassed anything that I'd ever felt before.

Once back inside our car, I told Jerry, "I'd really like to come back tomorrow. There are some things *I* would now like to ask." Jerry was delighted to make another appointment because he had more questions on his list as well.

About halfway through our allotted time on the following day, Jerry reluctantly relinquished the remaining minutes to me, and I asked Theo, "How can we more effectively achieve our goals?"

The answer came back: "Meditation and affirmations."

The idea of meditation didn't appeal to me at all, and I wasn't aware of anyone who practiced it. In fact, when I thought of the word, it brought to mind people lying on beds of nails, walking on hot coals, standing on one foot for years, or begging for donations at the airport. So I asked, "What do you mean by *meditation?*"

The answer was short, and the words felt good as I heard them. "Sit in a quiet room. Wear comfortable clothing, and focus on your breathing. As your mind wanders, and it will, release the thought and focus upon your breathing. It would be good for you to do it together. It will be more powerful."

"Could you give us an affirmation that would be of value for us to use?" we asked.

"*I* [say your name] *see and draw to me, through divine love, those Beings who seek enlightenment through my process. The sharing will elevate us both now.*"

As the words flowed from Sheila/Theo, I felt them penetrate to the core of my being. A feeling of love flowed to me and through me like nothing I'd ever felt before. My fear was gone. Jerry and I both felt wonderful.

"Should we bring my daughter, Tracy, to meet you?" I asked.

"Yes, if it is her asking, but it is not necessary . . . for you, too, Esther, are a channel."

That statement made no sense to me at all. I couldn't believe that I could be this old (in my 30s), and not already know something like that, if it were true.

The tape recorder clicked off, and we both felt mild disappointment that our extraordinary experience was finished. Sheila's assistant asked us if we had one last question. "Would you like to know the name of your spiritual guide?" she asked.

I would have never asked that, for I had never heard the term *spiritual guide,* but it sounded like a good question. I liked the idea of guardian angels. So I said, "Yes, please, could you tell me the name of my spiritual guide?"

Theo said, "We are told it will be given to you directly. You will have a clairaudient experience, and you will know."

What is a clairaudient experience? I wondered, but before I could ask my question, Theo said with a tone of finality, "God's love unto you!" and Sheila opened her eyes and sat up. Our extraordinary conversation with Theo had ended.

After Jerry and I left the house, we drove to a lookout point on the side of one of the Phoenix mountains and leaned against the car, looking off into the distance watching the sunset. We had no idea of the transformation that had taken place within us that day. We only knew that we felt wonderful.

When we returned home, I had two powerful new intentions:

I was going to meditate, whatever in the world *that* meant, and I was going to find out the name of my spiritual guide.

So, we changed into our robes, closed the curtains in the living room, and sat in two large wingback chairs, with an étagère between us. We'd been encouraged to do this together, but it felt odd, and the étagère helped to mask the strangeness for some reason.

I remembered Theo's instructions: *Sit in a quiet room, wear comfortable clothing, and focus on your breathing.* So we set a timer for 15 minutes, and I closed my eyes and began to breathe consciously. In my mind, I asked the question: *Who is my spiritual guide?* and then I counted my breath, in and out, in and out. Right away, my entire body felt numb. I couldn't distinguish my nose from my toes. It was a strange but comforting sensation, and I enjoyed it. It felt as if my body were slowly spinning even though I knew that I was sitting in a chair. The timer rang and startled us, and I said, "Let's do it again."

Once more, I closed my eyes, counted my breaths, and felt numb from head to toe. Again, the timer rang and startled us. "Let's do it again," I said.

So we set the timer for another 15 minutes, and again I felt numbness overtake my entire body. But this time, something, or someone, began to "breathe my body." From my vantage point, it felt like rapturous love, moving from deep inside my body outward. What a glorious sensation! Jerry heard my soft sounds of pleasure and later said that, to him, I appeared to be writhing in ecstasy.

When the timer went off and I came out of the meditation, my teeth chattered like never before. *Buzzed* would be a better word for the experience. For nearly an hour, my teeth buzzed as I tried to relax back into my normal state of awareness.

At that time, I didn't realize what had happened, but I know now that I'd experienced my first contact with Abraham. While I didn't know *what* had happened, I did know that whatever it was—*it was good!* And I wanted it to happen again.

So Jerry and I made the decision to meditate every day for 15 minutes. I don't think we missed a day in the next nine months. I felt the numbness, or feeling of detachment, each time, but nothing else extraordinary happened during our meditations. And then, right before Thanksgiving of 1985, while meditating, my head began to move gently from side to side. For the next few days, during meditation, my head would move in that gentle flowing motion. It was a lovely sensation that sort of felt like flying. And then, on about the third day of this new movement, during meditation, I realized that my head was not randomly moving about, but it was as if my nose was spelling letters in the air. "M-N-O-P" is what I realized it was.

"Jerry," I shouted, "I'm spelling letters with my nose!" And with those words, the rapturous feelings returned. Goose bumps covered my body from head to toe as this nonphysical energy rippled through my body.

Jerry quickly took out his notebook and began writing down the letters, as my nose wrote them in the air: "I AM ABRAHAM. I AM YOUR SPIRITUAL GUIDE."

Abraham has since explained to us that there are many gathered there with "them." They refer to themselves in the plural because they're a collective consciousness. They've explained that, in the beginning, the words "I am Abraham" were spoken through me only because my expectation for my spiritual guide was singular, but that there are *many* there with them, speaking, in a sense of the word, with one voice, or a consensus of thought.

To quote Abraham: *Abraham is not a singular consciousness as you feel that you are in your singular bodies. Abraham is a collective consciousness. There is a nonphysical stream of consciousness, and as one of you asks a question, there are many, many points of consciousness that are funneling through what feels to be the one perspective (because there is, in this case, one human, Esther, who is interpreting or articulating it), so it appears singular to you. We are multidimensional and multifaceted and certainly multiconscious.*

Abraham has since explained that they're not whispering words into my ears, which I am then repeating for others, but instead they're offering blocks of thoughts, like radio signals, which I'm receiving at some unconscious level. I then translate those blocks of thoughts into the physical word equivalent. I "hear" the words as they're spoken through me, but during the translation process itself, I have no awareness of what is coming, or any time for recollection of what has already come to me.

Abraham explained that they had been offering these blocks of thoughts to me for quite some time, but I was so strictly trying to follow Theo's instructions—which said, "When your mind wanders, and it will, release the thoughts and focus on your breathing"—that whenever one of these thoughts would begin, I would release it as quickly as possible and focus back upon my breathing. I guess the only way they could get through to me was to spell letters in the air with my nose. Abraham says that those wonderful sensations that rippled through my body when I realized that I was spelling words was the joy they felt upon my recognition of our conscious connection.

Our communication process evolved rapidly over the next few weeks. The spelling of letters in the air with my nose was a very slow process, but Jerry was so excited about this clear and viable source of information that he would often wake me up in the middle of the night to ask Abraham questions.

But then, one night I felt a very strong sensation moving through my arms, hands, and fingers, and my hand began thumping on Jerry's chest as we lay in bed together watching television. As my hand continued to thump, I felt a very strong impulse to go to my IBM Selectric typewriter; and as I put my fingers on the keyboard, my hands began moving quickly up and down the keys as if someone were quickly discovering what this typewriter was all about and where the specific letters were placed. And then my hands began to type: Every letter, every number, again and again. And then the words began to take form on the paper: *I am Abraham. I am your spiritual guide. I am here to work with you. I love you. We will write a book together.*

We discovered that I could put my hands on the keyboard and then relax, much in the same way that I did during meditation, and that Abraham would then answer questions about anything that Jerry would ask. It was an amazing experience. They were so intelligent and so loving and so available! Anytime, day or night, they were there to talk to us about anything we wanted to discuss.

Then, one afternoon, while driving on a Phoenix freeway, I felt a sensation in my mouth, chin, and neck, similar to the familiar feeling of getting ready to yawn. It was a very strong impulse, so strong I couldn't stifle it. We were rounding a corner between two big trucks, and both of them seemed to be crossing the line into our lane at the same time, and I thought for a moment that they were going to drive right over the top of us. And in that very moment, the first words that Abraham spoke through my mouth burst out, "Take the next exit!"

We exited the freeway and parked in a lot underneath an overpass, and Jerry and Abraham visited for hours. My eyes were closed tightly, and my head moved up and down rhythmically as Abraham answered Jerry's stream of questions.

How is it that this wonderful thing has happened to me? At times, as I think about it, I can hardly believe that it's true. It seems like the kind of thing that fairy tales are made of—almost like making a wish as you rub the magic lantern. At other times, it seems like the most natural, logical experience in the world.

Sometimes I can barely remember what life was like before Abraham came into our lives. I have, with few exceptions, always been what most would call a happy person. I had a wonderful childhood, with no major childhood traumas; and along with two other sisters, I was born to kind and loving parents. As I mentioned, Jerry and I had been blissfully married for about four years, and I was, in every sense, living happily ever after. I wouldn't have described myself as someone filled with unanswered questions. In fact, I really wasn't asking many questions at all, and I hadn't formulated any strong opinions about much of anything.

Jerry, on the other hand, was filled with passionate questions. He was a voracious reader, always looking for tools and techniques that he could pass along to others to help them live more joyous lives. I've never known anyone who wants more to help others live successful lives.

Abraham has explained that the reason why Jerry and I are the perfect combination for doing this work together is because Jerry's powerful desire summoned Abraham, while my absence of opinions or angst made me a good receiver for the information that Jerry was summoning.

Jerry was so enthusiastic, even in his first interactions with Abraham, because he understood the depth of their wisdom and the clarity of their offering. And throughout all these years, his enthusiasm for Abraham's message hasn't waned in the least. No one in the room ever enjoys what Abraham has to say more than Jerry.

In the beginning of our interactions with Abraham, we didn't really understand what was happening, and we had no real way of knowing whom Jerry was talking with, but it was still thrilling and amazing and wonderful—and weird. It seemed so strange that I was certain that most people I knew wouldn't understand; they probably wouldn't even *want* to understand. As a result, I made Jerry promise that he would tell no one about our amazing secret.

I guess it's now obvious that Jerry didn't keep that promise, but I'm not sorry about that. There's nothing that either of us would rather do than be in a room filled with people who have things they'd like to discuss with Abraham. What we hear most often, from people who meet Abraham through our books, videos, audio series, workshops, or Website, is: "Thank you for helping me remember what I've somehow always known," and "This has helped me tie together all the pieces of truth that I've found along the way. This has helped me make sense of everything!"

Abraham doesn't seem interested in forecasting our future, as a fortune-teller might, although I believe that they always know what our future holds, but instead they're teachers who guide us from wherever we are to wherever we want to be. They've explained to us that it's not their work to decide what we should want, but it *is* their work to assist us in achieving whatever we desire. In Abraham's words: *Abraham is not about guiding anyone toward or away from anything. We want you to make all your decisions about your desires. Our only desire for you is that you discover the way to <u>achieve</u> your desires.*

My favorite thing that I've ever heard spoken about Abraham came to us from a teenage boy who had just listened to a recording in which Abraham was addressing some questions that teens had been asking. The boy said, "At first, I didn't believe that Esther was really speaking for Abraham. But when I heard the tape, and heard Abraham's answers to these questions, I then knew that Abraham was real, because there was no judgment. I don't believe that any person could be so wise, so fair, and without judgment."

For me, this journey with Abraham has been more wonderful than I can find words to explain. I adore the sense of Well-Being I've achieved from what I've learned from them. I love how their gentle guidance always leaves me with a feeling of self-empowerment. I love seeing the lives of so many of our dear friends (and new friends), improving through the application of what Abraham has taught them. I love having these brilliant and loving Beings pop into my head whenever I ask, always ready and willing to assist in our understanding of something.

(As an aside, several years after our meeting with Sheila and Theo, Jerry looked up the name *Theo* in our dictionary. "The meaning of *Theo,*" he joyously announced to me, "is 'God'"! How perfect that is! I smile as I reflect back on that wonderful day, which was such an extraordinary turning point for us. There I was, worried about interacting with evil, when I was, in fact, on my way to having a conversation with God!)

(From *Ask and It Is Given,* Hay House, 2004)

John Holland

Jack Foley

John Holland is an internationally renowned psychic medium and teacher who lectures, demonstrates, and reads for private clients; and who has spent more than 20 years developing his abilities. He has dedicated his life to personal development, which inspires him to teach others how to reconnect with their natural spiritual abilities with integrity and tap into their own unlimited resources.

John has been featured on The History Channel, A&E, *Unsolved Mysteries,* and in numerous articles; as well as becoming a familiar voice on radio stations throughout the world. He's the author of *Born Knowing, Psychic Navigator,* and *Power of the Soul.*

Website: **www.JohnHolland.com**

Heaven's
Little Dancer

During her time on Earth, Jennifer was often called "a little butterfly angel." She had such a spark inside of her that the five-year-old seemed to be illuminated from the inside out, and her spirit couldn't be kept still. This kid wanted to fly.

Of course, I didn't know anything about this special little girl until I "met" her during an appointment with her mother, Melinda, a hospital worker from California.

For more than a year, Melinda had been thinking about consulting a medium, and then she heard about me from a friend when I lived in Los Angeles.

"In my mind, I thought I was having visions of my little girl, but I couldn't be sure," she says now. "Was I losing my mind? I needed someone I could trust to tell me how I could find something so precious that I refused to believe was lost forever."

Our meeting actually began during a brief conversation that I felt compelled to have with Melinda before we shook hands. Usually I had an assistant set up my appointments, but something was telling me to call this woman myself—someone was actually insisting that I do so.

About one minute into our brief introduction via telephone, I saw a little girl who had only been gone for a short time. "Melinda, did you lose a daughter?" I asked her.

The sharp intake of breath was my answer. It turned out that Melinda's daughter had died after a kidney operation went terribly wrong, leaving her on life support for two days before her parents made the heartbreaking decision to allow her to pass on.

"She's standing over her brother," I continued. "She just loves him so much."

As I said this, Melinda told me that she glanced next to her, where her son was quietly playing.

A month later, I had the pleasure of meeting Melinda. We sat down in my office, and suddenly I felt a link to an elderly man with a warm face full of laugh lines. "Melinda, I think I have your grandfather here, and he's standing with someone hiding behind his leg. In fact, she loves to play hide-and-seek." I smiled because I knew it had to be the little girl again. "She's telling me that her name begins with a *J*."

Melinda confirmed that her beloved daughter's name was Jennifer. Next, I heard a *clackity-clackity-clack* sound. I thought that perhaps Jennifer had liked to tap dance, but her mother simply laughed, wiped away a couple of tears, and explained that the girl had a favorite pair of shoes that tapped when she ran.

"She called them her 'clackity-clack shoes,' and they were her favorites. We buried her in them," Jennifer's mom said, choking back a sob.

"The pain and the confusion of that time is gone," I assured her mother. "Right now, I see Jennifer dancing in her favorite yellow dress. In fact, she's prancing around on the Other Side like she owns the place."

"Is . . . is my baby okay? Is she in pain anymore?" Melinda asked. This was truly the reason she'd come to see me—she needed to put her mind at rest because she couldn't get that last sight of her little girl hooked up to all those tubes out of her mind.

"Jennifer is healthy, happy, and free," I said, and Melinda's face took on a luminous quality. Suddenly, I knew where little Jennifer got her spark. "I want you to know that your daughter's okay. Nothing can hurt her anymore."

Melinda mouthed "Thank you" and looked up at the sky.

"Wait, Mom. Now Jennifer is actually acting very boisterous—she wants me to mention May 9 to you. Does that have any special meaning?" I asked.

At first I couldn't hear Melinda's reply because Jennifer was giggling so loudly.

"I can't believe it!" Melinda finally proclaimed and then settled back on the couch to tell me a story. It seems that on May 9, a few weeks before her fatal operation, a platter of cupcakes was delivered to the kindergarten class to celebrate Jennifer's birthday.

The teacher hugged Melinda's daughter and told the class, "It's Jennifer's special day, so let's eat our cupcakes and give her our best wishes." (She later called Melinda to tell her that the cupcakes were actually for another Jennifer in a different class!)

When Jennifer came home, she sheepishly told the story to her mom. "It was so silly because Teacher thought it was my birthday today!" she admitted. "I know it was wrong, Mommy, but you know how much I love cupcakes. For me, it did turn into a very special day."

Her mother let her off the hook, and her family deemed May 9 Jennifer's second birthday, or her "very special day." When a smiling Jennifer was tucked into bed that night, her parents had to chuckle at the whole thing. Little did they know that a month later, life would take an unfair turn. . . .

During her 36 hours on life support, Melinda's own mother came to visit her granddaughter. "Soon you'll be able to fly far, far away, but you'll always be our little angel butterfly," she whispered, clutching the little girl's warm hand.

Her family was taking a short break from a vigil at the hospital when Jennifer crossed over. At the exact moment of her passing, her sister, Lisa, stopping running around the yard, looked at a white butterfly in the sky and exclaimed, "See, it's my sister! My sister!"

"Melinda," I said during our reading, "I don't want you to think that you're crazy, because you've actually been seeing Jennifer around the house. She's telling me that she visits you often and is still a vital part of the family."

I could see the stress and pressure leave Melinda's face. It was almost as if I were giving her the okay to believe. "John, the other day I was reading a book in my living room," she said, "and it looked like someone had her face pressed against the glass from the outside. I saw a little girl waving to me. Then I went outside and no one was there," she told me. "Also, everywhere I go, I always see butterflies. For example, the other night, my husband and I took a walk, and this beautiful blue tropical butterfly unlike any I've ever seen in our area settled on the tip of his shoe. It even let my husband transfer it to his hand. It was as if it belonged to us."

I nodded. "Lisa has also seen Jennifer. Right now, Jennifer is saying hello to her sister and brother, too. She wants you to know that she talks to both of them."

"Her little brother says that he keeps hearing sounds. I even thought his ear tubes were blocked, but the doctor said they aren't," Melinda said. "And Lisa was on a field trip the other day when a butterfly landed on her finger and stayed there for a really long time. Everyone thought it was amazing."

Now Jennifer was telling me something so great that I knew I had to share it with her mother. "Your daughter says she loves giving hugs to her brother and sister. And now she can't wait to hug her new baby brother," I told her mother who finally shook her head.

"I'm sorry, John. You're finally wrong here. Jennifer only has one brother," she said.

"Darling, I think what your daughter is telling me is that you're pregnant," I gently said.

Melinda's purse fell to the floor—then she began to laugh and shake her head. "There's absolutely no way that I'm pregnant, but it's a lovely idea," she said.

"Well, let me know what happens," I said. At that moment, Jennifer gave me a little wink, and I just knew that another child would soon be entering this family and that it would be a boy. Of course, Melinda was here to talk about the little girl that she'd lost, so I let my focus return to her. "Jennifer wants me to say that she loves her balloons and notes. She says to tell you that she knows you're not planning to do balloons this year, but really wants them, too. Does this mean anything to you?"

Melinda excitedly nodded and said, "Every year since her death, we celebrate Jennifer's birthday by releasing white balloons in the air with messages stuffed inside them saying how much we love her. This year I ordered butterflies from a local farm that breeds and raises them. I invited each child in Jennifer's class to come to our house and release one butterfly into the sky."

"Well, Mom, your little girl loves that idea, but she says that she also wants her balloons because she looks forward to them."

Melinda's eyes misted over again and she vowed, "There will definitely be balloons this year."

Later she told me, "I left your office feeling like a weight had been lifted off my chest. I finally had confirmation that Jennifer was happy and healthy. She was a joyous little girl once again, and I know she's still a big part of our family."

Jennifer is also a very smart cookie. "A week after I came back from Los Angeles, I found out that I was pregnant," Melinda confirmed, and eight months later, a beautiful baby boy joined the family.

After the baby was born, Melinda was standing outside on the front lawn when a longtime friend, who didn't believe any of what Melinda and I had discussed, chose to make a visit. Suddenly, the woman was standing in the center of the lawn in total silence. When Melinda asked what was going on, the woman could only whisper, "I just saw the strangest thing. An image of a little girl who reminds me of Jennifer just ran up behind you and threw her arms around your legs. I saw her do it!"

"This was always Jennifer's way of greeting me in the morning," Melinda reported to me. "Another night, my son saw a ball of light dancing in the front yard. Little Matthew ran in to tell me that he thought it was his sister. I could only smile, because our little angel butterfly was watching over her family. I don't question these sightings anymore, John. Talking to you brought me so much comfort because nobody can ever take my little girl away. Her wings have allowed her to fly high, but she can also come home again."

After such an emotional reading with Melinda, I went to the beach to clear my own head. I was the only one out there, and I sat down in the sand to watch a brilliant sunset. As I stared into the horizon, I couldn't help but notice something slowly approaching on shore. As I walked toward it, I couldn't believe my eyes. It was a single red balloon. Somehow I feel it was a thank-you sent special delivery . . . compliments of Jennifer.

(From *Born Knowing*, Hay House, 2003)

Immaculée Ilibagiza

Lisa Kahane

Immaculée Ilibagiza was born in Rwanda and studied electronic and mechanical engineering at the National University. She lost most of her family during the 1994 genocide. Four years later, she emigrated to the United States and began working for the United Nations in New York City. She is establishing the Ilibagiza Foundation to help others heal from the long-term effects of genocide and war. Immaculée lives in Long Island with her husband, Bryan Black, and their two children, Nikeisha and Bryan, Jr. She is the author, with Steve Erwin, of *Left to Tell: Discovering God Amidst the Rwandan Holocaust.*

FORGIVING
THE LIVING

Miraculously, I survived the slaughter in Rwanda. For 91 days, I, along with seven other women, had huddled silently together in the cramped bathroom of a local pastor's home while hundreds of machete-wielding killers hunted for us.

It was during those endless hours of unspeakable terror that I discovered the power of prayer, eventually shedding my fear of death and forging a profound and lasting relationship with God. I emerged from my bathroom hideout having truly discovered the meaning of unconditional love—a love so strong that I was able to seek out and forgive my family's killers. . . .

⌒

I knew that my family was at peace, but that didn't ease the pain of missing them. And I couldn't shake the crippling sorrow that seized my heart whenever I envisioned how they'd been killed. Every night I prayed to be released from my private agony, from the nightmares that haunted my sleep and troubled my days. It took a while, but as always, God answered my prayers. This time, He did so by sending me a dream unlike any I've ever had.

I was in a helicopter flying over my family's house, but I was trapped in a dark cloud. I could see Mom, Dad, and my brothers Damascene and Vianney high above me, standing in the sky and bathed in a warm, white light that radiated tranquility. The light intensified and spread across the sky until it engulfed the dark cloud hiding me. And suddenly, I was with my family again. The dream was so real that I reached out and felt the warmth of their skin, the gentleness of their touch. I was so happy that I danced in the air.

Damascene was wearing a crisp white shirt and blue trousers. He looked at me with a joyful glow and gave me his brilliant smile. My mother, father, and Vianney stood behind him, holding hands and beaming at me. "Hey, Immaculée, it's good to see that we can still make you happy," my beautiful brother said. "You've been gloomy far too long and must stop all this crying. Look at the wonderful place we're in . . . can you see how happy we are? If you continue to believe that we're suffering, you'll force us to return to the pain we've left behind. I know how much you miss us, but do you really want us to come back and suffer?"

"No, no, Damascene!" I cried out, as tears of joy poured from my eyes. "Don't come back here! Wait for me there, and I will come join you all. When God is done with me in this life, I will come to you."

"We'll be here waiting, dear sister. Now heal your heart. You must love, and you must forgive those who have trespassed against us."

My family slowly receded into the sky until they disappeared into the heavens. I was still hovering over my house, but I was no longer in a dark cloud . . . and no longer in a helicopter. I was flying like a bird above my village, above the pastor's house and the French camp, above all the forests and rivers and waterfalls of my beautiful country—I was soaring above Rwanda.

I felt so liberated from grief and gravity that I began to sing for joy. I sang from my heart, the words tumbling happily from my mouth. The song was "Mwami Shimirwa," which in the language of Kinyarwanda means "Thank You, God, for love that is beyond our understanding."

From that night onward, my tears began to dry and my pain eased. I never again agonized over the fate of my family. I accepted that I would always mourn and miss them, but I'd never spend another moment worrying about the misery they'd endured. By sending me that dream, God had shown me that my family was in a place beyond suffering.

He'd also shown me that I had to make a trip to my village.

A few weeks later, Colonel Gueye, the Senegalese officer responsible for a number of the UN peacekeepers who'd come to Rwanda to help stabilize the country, gave me a lift home, and we drove cross-country. The landscape of my youth no longer saddened me; rather, I was heartened by the warm memories stirred by the sights and sounds around me. I wandered with friends through my mother's banana plantation and my father's mountainside coffee crops. I told my aunts that if they weren't afraid of going outside, they could harvest the crops to support themselves.

Aunt Jeanne told me not to worry about her being afraid: She was getting a gun and would learn how to shoot. "Next time I'll be ready," she said.

Next time, I thought with a heavy sigh.

I went to my old house to visit my mom and Damascene. I knelt by their graves and told them all that had happened since I'd last seen them. I told them about my job and what I planned to do in the future. I missed seeing their faces and hearing their voices, and I wept. But this time, my tears were a release, not a sorrow.

And then it was time to do what I'd come to do.

I arrived at the prison late in the afternoon and was greeted by Semana, the new burgomaster of Kibuye. Semana had been a teacher before the genocide, as well as a colleague and good friend of my dad's—he was like an uncle to me. Four of his six children had been killed in the slaughter, and I told him he must have faith that his little ones were with God.

"I can see how much the world has changed; the children now comfort the parents," he replied sadly.

As burgomaster, Semana was a powerful politician in charge of arresting and detaining the killers who had terrorized our area. He'd interrogated hundreds of Interahamwe (the Hutuextremist militia) and knew better than anyone which killers had murdered whom.

And he knew why I'd come to see him. "Do you want to meet the leader of the gang that killed your mother and Damascene?"

"Yes, sir, I do."

I watched through Semana's office window as he crossed a courtyard to the prison cell and then returned, shoving a disheveled, limping old man in front of him. I jumped up with a start as they approached, recognizing the man instantly. His name was Felicien, and he was a once-successful Hutu businessman whose children I'd played with in primary school. He'd been a tall, handsome man who always wore expensive suits and had impeccable manners. I shivered, remembering that it had been his voice I'd heard calling out my name when the killers searched for me at the pastor's. Felicien had hunted me.

Semana pushed Felicien into the office, and he stumbled onto his knees. When he looked up from the floor and saw that I was the one who was waiting for him, the color drained from his face. He quickly shifted his gaze and stared at the floor.

"Stand up, killer!" Semana shouted. "Stand up and explain to this girl why her family is dead. Explain to her why you murdered her mother and butchered her brother. Get up, I said! Get up and tell her!" Semana screamed even louder, but the battered man remained hunched and kneeling, too embarrassed to stand and face me.

His dirty clothing hung from his emaciated frame in tatters. His skin was sallow, bruised, and broken, and his eyes were filmed and crusted. His once-handsome face was hidden beneath a filthy, matted beard; and his bare feet were covered in open, running sores.

I wept at the sight of his suffering. Felicien had let the devil enter his heart, and the evil had ruined his life like a cancer in his soul. He was now the victim of his victims, destined to live in torment and regret. I was overwhelmed with pity for the man.

"He looted your parents' home and robbed your family's plantation, Immaculée. We found your dad's farm machinery at his house, didn't we?!" Semana yelled at Felicien. "After he killed Rose and Damascene, he kept looking for you . . . he wanted you dead so he could take over your property. Didn't you, pig?" Semana shouted again.

I flinched, letting out an involuntary gasp. Semana looked at me, stunned by my reaction and confused by the tears streaming down my face. He grabbed Felicien by the shirt collar and hauled him to his feet. "What do you have to say to her? What do you have to say to Immaculée?"

Felicien was sobbing. I could feel his shame. He looked up at me for only a moment, but our eyes met. I reached out, touched his hands lightly, and quietly said what I'd come to say.

"I forgive you."

My heart eased immediately, and I saw the tension release in Felicien's shoulders before Semana pushed him out the door and into the courtyard. Two soldiers yanked Felicien up by his armpits and dragged him back toward his cell. When Semana returned, he was furious.

"What was that all about, Immaculée? That was the man who murdered your family. I brought him to you to question . . . to spit on if you wanted to. But you forgave him! How could you do that? Why did you forgive him?"

I answered him with the truth: "Forgiveness is all I have to offer."

(From *Left to Tell*, Hay House, 2006)

Loretta LaRoche

Andreew Brilliant

Loretta LaRoche, the best-selling author of *Life Is Short—Wear Your Party Pants* and *Squeeze the Day*, among other works, is an internationally renowned author and stress-management consultant who advocates humor, optimism, and resiliency as coping mechanisms. She uses her wit and wisdom to help people learn how to take stress and turn it into strength, and how to see themselves as the survivors of their own lives—that is, to find the "bless in the mess." Loretta is a favorite with viewers of her six PBS specials, as well as on the lecture circuit, where she presents an average of 100 talks per year. She lives in Plymouth, Massachusetts.

Website: **www.LorettaLaroche.com**

You Never Know . . .

When I was growing up, one of my mother's favorite expressions was "You never know." We'd have to clean the house every Saturday, because . . . "You never know." If we were in the midst of enjoying a wonderful meal, we had to make sure there were leftovers, because . . . "You never know." Small pieces of wax paper were saved, along with brown string and empty egg cartons, because . . . well, you know.

I kept trying to understand what it was that we didn't know but needed to know. It was certainly enough to make a child anxious. Perhaps that was the point. After all, we *did* have fire drills at school, and we *were* in the midst of the Cold War—we were even taught to hide under our desks in case of a nuclear attack. Or what if a meteorite was going to hit the earth, which was something that our third-grade science teacher, Mr. Funkhauser, told us could happen.

Maybe my mother knew that something bad was going to happen and we had to get ready. I used to ask her, but she would always counter with, "Someday you'll see." See what? *What* was I going to see?

I could deal with most of it, but I really had a hard time not being able to wear my patent-leather shoes until Easter—especially since we'd bought them in February. The only thing I was allowed to do was put Vaseline on them so they wouldn't crack. Isn't that a thrill? I kept begging to wear them, but my mother kept giving me the same answer—you know what she said, don't you?

The thing that really pushed me over the edge was the underwear. She always bought me the most hideous underpants. She said that they were on sale and the clerk told her they wouldn't wear out. Well, I don't know what the clerk thought I was going to be doing—maybe going into a mine shaft and not coming out for a month? Why did they have to be so sturdy? Why couldn't I just have the kind that were pretty and feminine, with little flowers and lace?

Well, my mother finally had a weak moment and bought me a pair. I was ecstatic until she said the usual: that I couldn't wear them often because . . . "You never know." She added that they were going to be my "party pants." That didn't ease the pain. How many parties does a nine-year-old go to? It's not as if I were a movie star or something. So the pants stayed in the drawer surrounded by their ugly step-underpants. I probably got to wear them twice. I still have them; they just don't fit.

As an adult, I now have a much better understanding of what "You never know" meant to my mother and why she needed to say it so often. She and my grandparents lived through the Depression and World War II. These folks have been called "The Greatest Generation" due to their amazing resiliency. They were the product of a world in which the economic present was bleak and the future was scary. As a result, my mother's ability to enjoy things fully was tinged with dread and guilt.

For example, she had a wonderful set of hand-painted dishes that had been in the family since I was 14. We carried them home from a vacation in Bermuda and almost broke our backs, they were so heavy. They were a 12-piece setting, each hand-painted with a blue cornflower. Each one was different. Now, frankly, I think the whole thing was a little crazy. Who cared about the fact that each one was different? What was going to happen—were we all going to compare plates, and say, "Oh, look, yours doesn't have a stem?"

My mother thought they were incredibly special. And why not? She'd bought them with her hard-earned money, something she pointed out over and over. They sat in the china closet, waiting for those special individuals my mother felt were deserving enough to eat off them. We, the village idiots, weren't good enough to eat on these superior dishes under ordinary circumstances. Every once in a while she'd remind me that she was leaving them to me. For a long time, I really relished the thought. One day, two years ago, she asked, "Do you want the dishes?" I thought, *You must be kidding. . . .* My idea of dinnerware now is some plastic plates to eat takeout on.

I don't think my mother was mean, and I don't think she really thought her family was unworthy of the good plates. She was simply living the life she was taught to live. We all inherit a point of view from our families and our societies that, for better or worse, creates who we are and what we believe. We often inherit concepts about life but don't really understand why.

One of my favorite stories concerns a woman who was in her kitchen preparing a roast beef for dinner. Her young daughter was watching her make the meal, and the girl asked, "Mommy, why did you cut the ends off the roast beef?"

And the mother told her: "Honey, that's just the way you prepare it."

"But why?"

And the mother had to think about it for a second and acknowledged, "You know, I'm not sure why. It's the way my mother did it, and I'm sure she had a good reason."

"Let's ask Grandma."

So the woman called her mother and asked why she cut the ends off the roast beef. The older woman had to admit that she didn't really know why she did it either, but she did it because that's the way *her* mother prepared a roast beef.

So they called the old woman, the child's great-grandmother, who was now in her 90s, and asked her why she cut the ends off the roast beef before cooking it.

"Well," the old lady said, "it's because I didn't have a roasting pan big enough to hold it."

Many of us have inherited a scarcity mentality from our parents, or a mentality that says we shouldn't celebrate and use the good china in our everyday lives. But like the woman who cooked the roast beef, we have to look beyond what we've been brought up with to try to find our own paths to a happy life.

Certainly, we need to save for the future, and not simply waste things or indulge ourselves with material goods we don't need. But we should never wait to celebrate life only on special occasions. We need to bring a feeling of celebration into our lives *every day*. We haven't got time to wait. As I often say to my audiences and workshop members about the precariousness of life: "Nobody is getting out of here alive."

When I make this statement, a lot of people laugh, but I also know they're thinking, *Why is she being so morbid? This is supposed to be funny.* And yet, when we truly acknowledge our mortality, we're forced to live in the present because we understand that this is the only thing that's certain. It forces us to focus on the things that are truly important, and allows us to put aside the things that aren't. It reminds us that what we "awfulize" about today will pass. The slow checkout line becomes a walk in the park. The traffic jam becomes a time to hear good music. And two extra hours at work aren't such a trial if you plan to be home in time to kiss your daughter good night.

We have a very short time on this planet, and we waste so many hours not really enjoying what time we have. So many of us seem to be waiting, waiting. . . .

Have you ever asked yourself: "What am I waiting for? What needs to be done before I can do the thing I'm postponing? What do I need to have before I can do it, and why?" or "Who am I waiting to get permission from?"

Believe me, no one's coming to give you permission—they're out having a good time.

(From *Life Is Short—Wear Your Party Pants,* Hay House, 2003)

Mike Lingenfelter

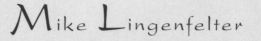

Mike Lingenfelter is an accomplished engineer, and a member of the Institute of Electrical and Electronic Engineers. He holds 17 patents for his work worldwide. Mike and his wife, Nancy, reside in Huntsville, Alabama. He's the author (with David Frei) of *The Angel by My Side: The True Story of a Dog Who Saved a Man . . . and a Man Who Saved a Dog.*

Dakota was Mike's very special golden retriever service dog, who possessed unique, lifesaving talents.

My Angel,
Dakota

It was 1994, and I expected my life to end soon. Two serious heart attacks and open-heart surgery had stripped away most of the pleasure I had in life. My doctors still held out hope for me, though. Their vision was that an energetic dog on a leash might motivate me to get out of the house and exercise. And so it was that a golden retriever named Dakota (whom I nicknamed Cody)—who'd been rescued from death himself—came to live with me and help me with my rehabilitative therapy. . . .

⌣

"Leave me alone!" I shouted to the small group that had gathered around me as I sprawled on the floor.

"Are you okay?" asked a female customer. "What can we do?"

My mind was racing: *Where am I? What am I doing here?* I'd already shoved a couple of nitroglycerin pills into my mouth, and I tried to speak more calmly to the concerned onlookers. "Just leave me alone—give my medication a chance to work."

I was having a severe angina attack, and it was just my luck that I happened to be in a very public place—the local Wal-Mart. Usually my wife, Nancy, helped me with the driving and kept an eye on me when I went out in public. This time I was just trying to run a quick errand, and I hadn't given much thought to any possible heart episodes. So here I was, alone and having to worry about how everyone around me might over- or underreact, either of which could cause me problems. I was so happy with the way things were going with Dakota and my return to public life after being ill that I sometimes overlooked the fact that I was still burdened with the possibility of a health crisis at any time.

This was one of those times.

The heart is pretty independent and does just about anything that it wants to do, good or bad. The good comes in the form of a long, healthy life. The bad results every time someone "just drops dead from a heart attack." Now I have unstable angina, which isn't a heart attack—but they both start out the same way, and no matter what they call it, it still hurts . . . a lot. And it scares me—I still live in fear every day that my next attack will be "the big one."

Meanwhile, back at Wal-Mart, I survived, and most of the customers went back to their shopping. I unwound from the fetal position, took a few deep breaths, and sat up.

The store manager kneeled in front of me. "What do you need?" he asked. "Can we call someone?"

"I think I'll be okay in just a few more minutes. Sorry for creating a scene."

"That's the least of our concerns. I'm just glad that you're okay," he said. "I gather that you're used to dealing with this."

"Yes, I'm sorry to say I am." What I didn't share with him was that I was also feeling sorry for myself—for my vulnerability, for my loss of independence, and for the embarrassment I caused myself. Dakota was doing his job as a therapy dog, and my mental health was making a comeback—but a physical event like this one undid a lot of that psychological healing. It made me think about the fact that my life would never really get back to normal.

Being reminded of how close to death I was at any given moment could be really depressing and scary. I couldn't escape that fear. Cody or no Cody, I still occasionally backslid into thinking about using that gun I'd bought. After all, I still couldn't work, and I continued to have these attacks once or twice a week, often in an embarrassingly public way. Nancy saw to it that I stayed busy with Dakota and our visits on behalf of Paws for Caring. That's what helped me fight back against the depression that unfortunately will always be there for me.

Working with kids was still the best prescription for my own well-being. There was a home and school for children with Down syndrome down the road from us. The kids went there for schooling and physical activities, ranging from walking to playing softball. Cody and I made this into a family event, with Nancy and my other dog, Abbey, joining us once a week throughout the summer. The children loved the dogs, and they helped motivate the kids to do a lot of different activities. It was great fun for Dakota and Abbey, too—after all, who plays ball better than a golden retriever?

I was still battling angina attacks. They could happen two or three times a day, or just once or twice a week. The doctors were trying to find the right drugs and the right dosages to help me control it, and over the first 18 months we were together, Cody witnessed hundreds of these painful episodes. He learned to crawl into bed with me or lie next to me on the floor, sometimes staying there for hours to help me fight through the attack. As my chest tied into a knot, I would squeeze him hard to shift my own pain. I know that he felt my pain, but he never flinched. There was nothing either of us could do, however, to keep these episodes from occurring.

One day in the fall of 1996, Dakota and I were visiting a school as part of Pet Awareness Week. Our veterinarian, Dr. Pat Choyce, had asked me to speak about animal-assisted therapy and service dogs. We were just starting our presentation when Cody started to act a little rambunctious. He was pawing at me and ignoring my instructions, acting as if he had a serious problem. I thought that maybe he was going to throw up or he needed to relieve himself. He'd never acted like this in public before, and, at the very least, I wanted to get him out of there to straighten him out. I was a little upset with him for making us leave in the middle of the program, but I apologized to our panel leader and took him off the stage.

I walked out the door of the auditorium and just as the door closed behind me, I felt a crushing, sharp pain in my chest and a shortness of breath. My knees buckled and I blacked out. When I came to, there were a lot of people around me, yelling and screaming. I took my medication and sat there for a while collecting myself as the medication went to work. Dakota, who had never left my side, was licking my arms and my face.

Dr. Choyce was there, too, watching this amazing animal work on me. "Maybe he was trying to tell you something," he said.

"You may have something there," I told him.

I looked at Cody. His eyes seemed to be bluish-gray, a color I'd never seen before. A few minutes later, they were back to their normal brown color. I decided that I was probably seeing this color change because I was still a little out of it.

Dr. Choyce drove me home, and we talked about this episode on the way. As I looked back over the past month or so, I could remember Dakota acting the same toward me each time I had an attack. Maybe I should have been paying closer attention to him. I talked to Nancy about it when I got home, and she pointed out that just a couple of days before, Cody had pawed at me and had gotten very agitated while I was lying on the couch. I told him to leave me alone, but he wouldn't let up. Minutes later, I had an attack. In my mind, I blamed him for making me mad enough to push me into a medical emergency.

Now I like to think that I'm a pretty smart person: I'm an engineer, I'm well educated, and I hold something like 17 patents. Yet I was reluctant to give Dakota credit for this ability because I just didn't think it was possible. But in my heart (so to speak), it slowly dawned on me that somehow Dakota was sensing when these attacks were about to occur.

I was at home the next time Cody exhibited this behavior. I was sitting at my desk, working at the computer, while he napped on the carpet. Suddenly, he transformed from a well-behaved, docile golden retriever into the medical caregiver from hell. Catching me completely by surprise, he nuzzled me and pushed his head up under my arm and into my leg. I got a little perturbed as he made me spill my cup of coffee all over my desk. Since I was now paying more attention to the coffee than to him, he pawed at me, put his paw first on my arm and then my leg, and gave me a little push, as if to say, "Hey! I'm not kidding!"

Finally, I realized what he was trying to tell me. Cody was trying to save my life! My life could end in the next few minutes—I could clean up the coffee later. If I were right about Dakota, if somehow he'd learned to sense when I was about to have an angina attack, then I figured that I ought to be able to do something with that warning. I took him seriously, and I swallowed my medication immediately. And sure enough, an angina attack followed. Since I felt this one coming quickly, I headed directly for my bed.

Cody didn't relax, which led me to believe that this attack was going to be a bad one. I began to get hot and started to sweat. I felt short of breath, and my heart was trying to pound its way out of my chest. I was helpless. I tried to cry out for Nancy, but I wasn't sure where she was, and Dakota wouldn't leave my side to go get her.

Clearly I wasn't in control—this dog was. He completely took charge, climbing up on my bed and looking me in the eye to reassure me that he was here. Then he turned one of those dog circles and laid down in front of me, putting his back against my chest, as if to say, "Here you go, hang on." I gave him a quick hug and said a little prayer: "Please God, let this one be short."

God had other plans. The pain suddenly crushed me, twisting my chest into a knot as it shot through my entire body. This was a feeling I'd come to know. Normally, when an attack struck me without any warning, it would knock me to the ground. But this time, thanks to Dakota, I was ready to deal with it. Even with that advance warning, the pain quickly drained my strength, and I had to work hard to concentrate so that the medication would take effect quickly.

I felt Cody's warm body against mine, and I grabbed ahold of him. In spite of the growing pain and my increasing heart rate, I sensed his steady breathing. By emulating his calm presence and synchronizing my breathing with his, I was able to control my respiration rate and keep from hyperventilating. But the pain got worse, and my bear-hugging pressure on Dakota increased. He seemed to understand, and as he had many times before, he stayed with me without showing any sign of the pain that I know I was causing him. The time passed, and my anguish became more bearable. Little by little, the weight was lifted from my chest, I could breathe without pain, and my heart rate returned to something resembling normal.

Throughout this entire ordeal, Cody didn't move or even make a sound. As my grip on him lessened, he turned and sympathetically began to lick my hands, arms, and face. This told me that I'd survived. I rested for a few hours to regain my strength. Some of my attacks can be more serious than others, but having a warning clearly helped. The episode was much less severe than usual, and a head start on my medication helped counteract the attack and lessen its effects, while also avoiding an accident or a fall.

How did Cody know? He was exhibiting classic "alerting" behavior, typical of seizure-alert dogs—pawing at, nuzzling, or jumping on the ill person. Some service dogs have been doing this for years, alerting their human partners about an imminent medical event, such as an epileptic seizure or diabetic emergency. I'd heard about this from some other people with service dogs—they told amazing stories of how their dogs would "alert on" them in a crisis. So I understood the principles and knew the terminology, but in all of my reading and work with doctors and service-dog owners, I hadn't heard or read about a dog alerting on someone with heart problems.

Questions filled my mind: What did Cody smell, sense, or hear? What was he thinking? How did he come to learn this behavior? What was it that finally got him to recognize what was happening to me? How did he make the leap to realizing that he could help me? And most important—did he *know* that he was saving my life? Because that's exactly what he was doing by helping me get the medication into my system in advance, just like all those seizure-alert dogs did with their people. And the support he was giving me by absorbing my crushing hugs and helping me breathe was a very big part of it as well.

On this day, Dakota gave me my freedom back.

I'd been living—and nearly dying—with these angina attacks for close to five years. I thought back on that time frame, and about all of those scary, unpredictable episodes I'd had, such as the one in Wal-Mart. I was vulnerable and dependent on other people to help me live my life, and I had to be careful about going out in public. But maybe I could begin to look at things differently.

Now that I knew what to look for, I almost wanted to have another attack soon so I could test this theory and see if Dakota would respond the same way again. You know what they say about being careful what you wish for: Two days later I was sitting in my recliner reading the paper when that big red furry paw came crashing through my sports page.

"Cody!" I snapped.

He took another swipe at me with that same paw. I didn't need to be told again. I took my pills and headed for the bedroom, literally hoping that I was about to have another attack. And I did. I had this very strange mix of pain and elation—I was hurting physically, of course, but it didn't seem quite as bad as it usually did. The medication was already at work. But something else was going on. I now had an alarm system for these attacks: a four-legged, 98-pound, reddish-gold alarm system. He was taking the job away from Nancy and others.

Our lives were changing once again, thanks to Dakota.

(From *The Angel by My Side,* Hay House, 2002)

Denise Linn

Meadow Linn

Denise Linn is an internationally renowned teacher in the field of self-development. She's the author of 17 books, including *If I Can Forgive, So Can You*; *The Soul Loves the Truth*; and *Four Acts of Personal Power*, which are available in 24 languages. Denise has appeared in numerous documentaries and television shows worldwide, gives seminars on six continents, and is the founder of the International Institute of Soul Coaching®, which offers professional certification programs in life coaching.

Website: **www.DeniseLinn.com**

GOOD-BYE, FATHER

There's a lull that occurs between the moment a traumatic event has occurred for a loved one and the moment you hear of it. Although in your soul you already know what's happened and have begun to mourn, the conscious part of you continues to experience life as usual for a little bit longer. Yet there's an imperceptible but tangible shift of awareness that occurs in between those two times—to me, it feels like the seconds between when you lose your balance and the instant you hit the ground. Even as you free-fall, you know in a moment that you're going to eventually crash.

You can sense this subtle shift of energy precisely before you answer the late night call with the news that changes your life forever. When the call came with the report about my father, for instance, I denied what my soul already knew was true.

"Denise, your dad is dying. Come back as soon as you can," one of my father's neighbors said urgently. I held the phone away from my ear and stared at it numbly. I couldn't believe what I'd just heard. My father had colon cancer, but I hadn't expected to receive that call so soon. Actually, I didn't expect to *ever* receive it. Even though he no longer played a big part in my daily life, somehow I thought he'd always be around.

Shaking myself out of my stupor, I immediately threw some clothes into a suitcase that was already partially packed. As I raced to the airport, I wondered if I'd subconsciously known that I'd need to be prepared even if I couldn't consciously face that truth.

At the terminal, I was told that it would take three flights to get from where I was teaching in central California to the small Oregon town where my father and his second wife lived. The first flight was bumpy, but I barely noticed the turbulence because my thoughts were far away. I leaned my head against the window and thought about my relationship with the man who was my father. We'd never been very close, especially after the sexual abuse that had occurred during my childhood.

The emotional scars and the shame of what he had done to me night after night in his bed when I was a little girl and my mother was in a mental hospital were still fresh. Even though it had occurred 40 years earlier, I could not forget that abuse. Yet despite those memories, I not only visited him many times over the years, but I also tried to establish deeper ties with him. Regardless of the open wounds from my childhood, I continued to yearn for a loving father-daughter relationship. As I sat on the plane to go see him, I feared that it may have been too late for that.

While the plane bounced around in the sky, I thought back on the two times I'd tried to talk to my father about what had occurred when I was a child. Both times he denied it and ended the conversation quickly by abruptly walking out of the room. Once I asked him if he thought that I'd made it up—somehow it was important to me to know what he felt. He didn't answer me, so I asked him again, "Do you think I'm lying?" Again, he didn't answer me but merely looked down at the floor. I suppose that was the closest I ever got to an apology.

After those failed attempts at coming to a resolution, we tried to carry on with an unspoken pact of silence. Nevertheless, the abuse suffused my awareness whenever I was with him—it was an invisible, but nonetheless rock-solid, wall that stood between us. Even when I wasn't thinking about it, my body reacted differently when I was around him. For example, just one of his most innocent little half-hugs would cause a wave of nausea to unexpectedly wash over me.

The emotional pain from the abuse just wouldn't heal. I didn't need to consciously think about the past in order for it to be there—it always lurked buried beneath the surface of my psyche, ready to uncoil and strike out at any moment. Despite how irrational it might have been, I continued to think that if only my father would admit what had happened and apologize for it, then my pain would go away and my wounds would instantly heal. I still strove for that ideal, even as I rode on the plane to my father's deathbed . . . maybe it wasn't too late! I had crazy visions of an apology and a reconciliation, even if it came in the final moments of his life.

I finally touched down at the small local airport in my father's town. A family member picked me up, and by the look on her face, I could tell that the news wasn't good. Indeed, she said, "I'm so sorry, Denise. You're too late—he died a few hours ago."

Her words didn't register at first. I couldn't quite believe that he wasn't alive anymore. "He can't be dead," I stated. "Where's his body? I want to see it."

"You can't. We've sent it to be cremated."

"If he's not cremated yet, then I can still go see it," I said adamantly. I didn't know why I wanted to see his body, but somehow it seemed important.

After much discussion back at his home, it was finally agreed that I could go see my father's body, which was being held in a warehouse-type building in the industrial area of town. When I arrived there, a troll-looking man behind the front desk scrutinized me with squinty eyes.

"I'm here to see the body of my father," I announced.

With the tone of authority bestowed upon people who have small jobs and like to feel important, he informed me that it wouldn't be possible.

"I *will* see my father's body," I quietly demanded, as I gave him a hard, penetrating look.

My obstinate determination seemed to shake him for a moment, but he recovered and said haughtily, "Okay, but don't say I didn't warn you."

I was escorted into a cold, harshly lit room, where it became clear why the troll at the front desk didn't want me to go in: My father, gray and lifeless, lay on a slab, and while he was partially covered with a sheet, his head and the exposed parts of his body were badly bruised. He didn't die of head injuries, but there were gashes and nicks on his head and face. He was a big man, and I think that he must have been difficult to carry—they must have dropped him several times while getting him into the warehouse.

I pulled up a crate and sat down next to him. For a while I just sat there . . . and then I reached up and put my hand in his. It was cold and yet strangely comforting. It was the first time I could remember that my stomach didn't tighten when we touched.

I started to talk out loud. I didn't care if anyone else heard me—I had a lot to get off my chest. "I'm so damn angry with you! Now that you're dead, you're never going to admit to abusing me. You're never going to apologize for what you did! And I'm mad that you died before this could be healed," I said, trembling as I spoke.

I was crying so hard that I was having trouble getting the words out, but I continued, "I don't even know why I'm saying this now, because I'm not even sure that I believe it, but I forgive you. I forgive you for taking advantage of me when I was small. I forgive you for the way you put Mother in the mental hospital. I forgive you for ignoring me when I was shot and for not helping me when I was struggling to try to get into college.

"I forgive you for telling me 'Good luck' when I called you and said that I needed to borrow some money to fix the hole in my aorta, even when I told you I'd die without surgery. But damn it! I forgive you for that, too!" I was shouting and not thinking rationally. Everything that I'd stored up for years erupted out of me, and although I was saying words of forgiveness, I didn't feel as if I were actually forgiving him because I was becoming more and more enraged. A lifetime of anger bubbled to the surface as I continued to list all the things I "forgave" him for.

Then I heard these words, which seemed to come from my dad: "All those years *you* kept hoping that I'd come forward to ask for your forgiveness, *I* kept hoping that you'd come forward and forgive me."

Suddenly the anger and sadness dropped away. My father was dead, but I'd heard his words almost as clearly as if he were still alive, and all of my anguish disappeared. I felt devoid of emotion; I was completely empty as I realized that all those years I'd been waiting for an apology, *he'd* been waiting for my forgiveness.

I had to take the first step . . . it had to start with me! In that moment, I let go of the resentment and anger I'd harbored for a lifetime. I just surrendered, and it drained out of me—I didn't have to hold on to any of it anymore. A sense of salvation and freedom filled me, as the room overflowed with the same shimmering golden light I'd experienced when I was shot at age 17. As I squeezed my father's hand tightly, it didn't feel cold anymore—I knew that I loved him and that he loved me. Wonderful forgotten memories from childhood flooded my being—of my father fixing the tire on my red bicycle, the day he pulled all of us through the snow on an old wooden sled, and how he used to toss my little two-year-old brother, Brand, into the air as he squealed with delight. I loved my dad . . . I really loved him.

I stood up and fully looked at him. For the first time I could remember, I really saw my father. In the past, I'd usually avoid looking into his eyes—but as I looked at him in that moment, I became aware of the pain and disappointment that had plagued this man during his life. I sensed his self-disgust for abusing his daughter, and I saw all of his unfulfilled dreams and heartaches. And I wept for him for the first time in my life.

Gently stroking his forehead, I said, "Good-bye, Father." I hadn't called him Father since I was a kid—I always called him by his first name, Dick, as it had seemed more appropriate. Now I was saying good-bye to someone else. I was saying good-bye to my father.

The lightness I experienced stayed with me long after I left the warehouse. Even at the memorial service we had a few weeks later, I felt joyous about the opportunity to celebrate Father's life. We created a "stage," told great stories about his life, and shared photos. It was the first time that my siblings—Heather, Gordon, Brand—and I had been together since we were children, and it felt like a kind of homecoming. Later we stood together outside to cherish the enormous rainbow that splashed across the sky. Even though it was a sad event, there was a lot of joy and love shared. . . .

(From *The Soul Loves the Truth,* Hay House, 2006)

Monique Marvez

Barry Smith

With a background as one of North America's most entertaining and engaging stand-up comics, **Monique Marvez** has taken audiences by storm for the last 15 years. Her stage demeanor and on-air presence are described as relatable and conversational; and her act has been described in the press as a cross between a Hispanic Bette Midler and a prettier, sexier Dr. Phil. Currently, she's the morning host on 100.7 Jack FM/San Diego's show, *Monique and the Man*.

In addition to hosting successful radio shows in Indianapolis and Southern California, Monique has also appeared on *Dick Clark's Rockin' New Year's Eve* live from South Beach, HBO's *Real Sex* as a relationship expert, and has been a guest on the *Montel* show and *The Other Half*.

Her first book, *Not Skinny, Not Blonde*, is being released in September 2007.

Website: **www.MoniqueMarvez.com**

God Made Me Funny and Smart!

The holiday season of 1971, when I was nine, my dad suffered a not-very-mild nervous breakdown. If my memory serves me right, we went to visit him in the psychiatric ward of Jackson Memorial Hospital in Miami on Christmas Day. When my mom led me into the common area, I had on a supercool long-sleeved red dress with gold chains that crisscrossed down the front, and black patent-leather go-go boots. I was aware that something bad had happened, but I had no way of knowing the full effects . . . and besides, I looked terrific.

The timing couldn't have been worse. In the middle of fourth grade, when everything finally all blew apart, I was the most popular girl at Scott Lake Elementary School. In spite of a few quirky things at home such as the fact that my dad was never there and my mom alternated between crying and doing the rosary, I was happy. I loved school and my teacher, Ms. Janine Pollard. She was the coolest! I loved her because she was the first person outside of my family who took a special interest in me. On picture day, she teased my hair in the back, and when she got her new gold Mercury Marquis, she took me out to the parking lot to show it to me.

Being a latchkey kid with nobody waiting at home, I would stay after school and help Ms. Pollard clean up. We would talk about life; by now, I was used to having adult conversations. My parents had been struggling with the inevitable collapse of their marriage, and because I was a precocious child, they both confided in me. I felt the weight of their sorrow.

My time with Ms. Pollard was fun and carefree; we talked about how everyone could be beautiful and smart if they set their minds to it, and she told me about her boyfriends. She was a loving, appropriate role model.

Under my teacher/friend's watchful eye, I grew my hair long, chose my outfits daily with care, and started to understand my own brand of charisma. She showed me that it didn't matter that I wasn't blonde or petite. Right before my dad's breakdown, I was whatever you feel before you're aware of "sexy." I was supremely confident and at ease with myself in every way. This would be the last time I felt like that.

By early February of 1972, my red dress and go-go boots had grown tight as I began to rapidly gain weight. The breakdown had a domino effect on my life: My dad was out of his mind and wanted out of the marriage. Our beautiful home was put up for sale, and I had to transfer to another fourth-grade class near my grandmother's. All of this was pretty terrible, but the worst part was having to leave Ms. Pollard.

When the Dade County Youth Fair was going on that spring, Ms. Pollard drove down to my grandmother's and picked me up. Other than riding the double Ferris wheel, it was one of the best days of my life. I can still see all of Miami splayed out below me. The terror I felt was surpassed by the gratitude I felt, knowing that I still mattered to her. She made a few comments about how it was a special day, but in general, she advised me to avoid junk food. I had put on a lot of weight since the last time she saw me and I could feel her concern, but she didn't make me feel ashamed. That is the magic of good intentions and love.

Before Ms. Pollard took me home, we went to the Red Diamond Inn on 37th Avenue and she ordered me a Shirley Temple to go with my pepperoni pizza. We lost touch, and the inn has been torn down and replaced with a chiropractic clinic, but on her birthday, November 9, I send her blessings and prayers.

On September 23, 1972, I turned ten years old, but nobody remembered until 8 P.M. My favorite aunt, Christy, called and went on about what a lousy *tia* (aunt) she was to have forgotten her only niece's birthday. My mom shrieked and ran into my bedroom, where I lay facedown on my bed. She tried to explain what a tough time it had been these last eight months. I knew it would be rude to yell "Duh!"

When I look back at that day, it seems bizarre to me how much happened between nine and ten. I'm grateful that although it all affected me, it wasn't about me. Still, I didn't feel much like celebrating, but my brand-new stepfather, Guillermo, ran out and got my favorite cake with meringue icing. We sang, blew out candles, ate double helpings, and went to bed late. I was a little chubby.

By my 11th birthday, Guillermo was gone and I was obese.

I started my fifth elementary school in six years, Sylvania Heights, and I met Shannon Murphy, who immediately became my best friend because she was nonjudgmental and didn't care that I was the new girl and fat; it was a bonus that she was the prettiest girl in school. Had it only been a year and a half since I was the cute, popular girl?

On our first meeting, Shannon was preparing to fight another girl named Barbara and asked me to hold her earrings so she could kick the snot out of her. They were fighting over a piece of Sarah Coventry jewelry. Shannon's parents were heavy drinkers, and she had a little bit of an anger problem.

Shannon and I rode bikes a lot, but usually it was to a destination of peace and relief like Burger King or the Winn-Dixie grocery store, where the candy bars were still a dime. Although I had a great friend and was quite active, I knew that my size was a problem that I couldn't deny much longer. . . .

Halloween of sixth grade was the official sounding of the bell in round one against fat: *The Thrilla with Vanilla.*

All of my friends were gathering at Henry Alonso's to ride over to the best haunted house in Miami. Henry was a year ahead of us, but he hung out with our group because he had a crush on Shannon. Henry was high-strung and whiny, and in spite of his feelings for Shannon, this only son and mama's boy had all the earmarks of a future queen.

Everyone piled in the car except the two of us. Henry's mother suggested that he sit in the remaining spot and that I sit on his lap.

He stomped his foot and said, "Why, because she's a girl? She's twice my size. She'll smush me!" Henry's mom told him to be a *caballero* (gentleman), and he pouted and threw himself into the car with a dramatic, defeated sigh.

I turned and started walking home.

Shannon shouted from inside the packed car for me to please come back, but I didn't.

My mother greeted me with: "Good, maybe you'll do something about your weight now. Your Aunt Isa and I are joining Weight Watchers tonight. You can come with us."

Thank God I wasn't in costume; it would have added weight *and* humiliation.

My Aunt Isa was actually my dad's cousin and only had about a dozen pounds to lose. She was a sexy man magnet, even if she'd gotten a little hippy, and she had a great sense of humor. It would be all right if she was there.

What was not all right was that I was 4'9" and weighed 119 pounds.

As my friends spun on rides and got scared out of their wits by college kids dressed as zombies, I was told that I'd be eating beets and dry tuna for lunch. Now that's a horrible, frightening Halloween!

The three of us went to Weight Watchers for a few months. One week I had the biggest loss. I was 20 pounds down and my pants were all huge, but my mom wasn't doing as well and hit a plateau, so we stopped going.

Weight: It always comes back and brings friends.

By the eighth grade and the failure of my parents' second marriage to each other, I was up to 140 pounds. When my parents were reunited between the fifth and sixth grades, it should have made me happy, but it didn't because they were never meant to be married the first time, so the second time around was even worse.

I wish it were not so that I've spent so much of my thought power trying to get my weight below my IQ. One of those two numbers stays the same forever.

It took getting out of school and a failed marriage to my high-school sweetheart, but I finally figured out the key to my happiness:

Focus on one (the IQ) and ignore the other. At 27, I became a successful stand-up comedian and started feeling a deep gratitude for all of the challenges life had presented me. That made for some great material!

My opening line is: "I'd rather be skinny and blonde, but instead, God made me funny and smart!"

(From *Not Skinny, Not Blonde,* Hay House, 2007)

Dr. Eric Pearl

Devon Cass

Dr. Eric Pearl, the best-selling author of *The Reconnection,* walked away from one of the most successful chiropractic practices in Los Angeles when he started witnessing miraculous healings. Since that time, he has committed himself to imparting the light and information of the Reconnective Healing process through extensive lectures and seminars about "The Reconnection."

Eric has appeared on numerous TV programs and has also presented to a full house at Madison Square Garden. Articles about his seminars have been featured in various publications, including *The New York Times.*

Website: **www.TheReconnection.com**

A LIFE-AFTER-
DEATH EXPERIENCE

Most mothers remember their first birthing experience as special and unique. Some women go through days of torturous labor. Others give birth in the woods or in the backseat of a taxi. My mother? She died on the delivery table while in labor with me.

But dying wasn't what bothered her. What bothered her was having to come back to life. . . .

When will this baby be born? she agonized. In the labor room, Lois Pearl, my mother, had been doing her breathing exercises and bearing down, bearing down . . . but nothing was happening. No baby. No dilation. Just pain and more pain, with the doctor popping in to check on her between delivering other babies. She tried not to cry out; she was determined not to make a scene. After all, this was a hospital. There were sick people here.

Still, the next time the doctor came around, my mother looked up at her pleadingly, and with tears streaming, asked, "Is this ever going to end?"

Concerned, the doctor placed one hand firmly on my mother's abdomen to see if I had "dropped" enough to be delivered. The doctor's face showed that she wasn't quite convinced that I had done so. But taking into account my mother's excruciating pain, the doctor turned toward the nurse and reluctantly said, "Take her in."

145

My mother was placed on a gurney and wheeled into the delivery room. As the doctor continued to press on her abdomen, my mother noticed that the room was suddenly filled with the sound of someone screaming very loudly. *Boy,* she thought, *that woman's making a real fool of herself!* Then she realized that she and the medical personnel were the only ones in the room—which meant that the screaming must be coming from her. She was making a scene, after all. That really bothered her.

"When is this going to end?"

The doctor gave her a comforting look and a short whiff of ether. It was like placing a Band-Aid on a severed limb.

"We're losing her . . ."

My mother could barely hear the voice over the roar of motors— huge motors, like something you'd find in a factory, not a hospital. They hadn't started off that loudly. The sound, accompanied by a tingling sensation, had begun around the soles of her feet. Then it began climbing up her body as if the motors were moving upward, getting louder and louder as they progressed, shutting off the feeling in one area before they moved to the next. Only numbness was left in their wake.

Above the sound of the motors, the pain of labor continued with glaring intensity.

My mother knew that she'd remember that pain for the rest of her life. Her female ob-gyn—a practical, no-nonsense, country-style M.D.—believed that women should experience the "full expression" of childbirth. Which meant no painkillers. Not even during delivery, unless you counted the merest whiff of ether at the peak of contraction.

Strangely, none of the doctors or nurses appeared distracted. Here was this thundering sound, yet nobody in the delivery room seemed to notice it. My mother wondered, *How could this be?*

So the motors, and the numbness they left behind, should have been a relief. But as they rumbled past my mother's pelvis to her waist, she was struck by what she knew would happen when they reached her heart.

We're losing her . . .

No! She was flooded with a sense of resistance. Pain or no pain, she didn't want to die—she imagined the people she loved in mourning.

But no matter how she struggled, the motors wouldn't reverse. They proceeded upward, numbing her an inch at a time, as if erasing her existence. She was powerless to stop them. As my mother came to this realization, something strange happened. Although she still didn't *want* to die, suddenly a peace overcame her.

Losing her . . .

The motors reached her sternum. Their roar filled her head.

And then she began to *rise*. . . .

It wasn't my mother's *body* that was rising into the air. It was what she could only think of as her *soul*. She was being drawn upward, gravitating purposefully *toward* something. She didn't look back. No longer conscious of her physical surroundings, she knew that she'd already left the delivery room and its motors behind. She kept rising, moving upward. And, although she had no conscious knowledge of life after death, or of anything "spiritual," for that matter, it was of little consequence. It doesn't require a spiritual background to recognize when your fundamental essence is leaving your body and beginning to rise. There can only be one explanation for that.

My mother's final realization from the delivery table was that, although she was leaving everything that was familiar behind, *she no longer minded*. This surprised her initially. As soon as she stopped fighting and "let go," her journey began. What came to her first was a feeling of overall peace, tranquility, and an absence of all worldly responsibilities. None of the worrisome details of everyday life were bogging her down. *No more fears of the unknown.* One by one, they were all melting away . . . and what a relief it was. What a *great* relief. As this was happening, a lighter feeling came over her, and she became aware of the fact that she was *floating*. She was feeling so light, with the melting away of all of these worldly responsibilities, that she rose to an even higher level. And so began my mother's ascent, only stopping to absorb knowledge of one kind or another.

She rose through a succession of different levels—she doesn't recall a distinct "tunnel," as some who have had similar experiences

147

have reported. What she did recall was that along the way she encountered "others." These were more than just "people." They were "beings," "spirits," and "souls" of those whose time had ended here on Earth. These "souls" spoke to her, although *spoke* may not be the most accurate word. The communication was nonverbal, a kind of thought transference that left no doubt as to what was being conveyed. Doubt did not exist here.

My mother learned that verbal language, as we know it, is not so much an *aid* to communication as it is a communication *barrier.* It's one of the hurdles we're given to master as part of our learning experience here on Earth. It's also part of what keeps us in the limited scope of understanding in which we are to function in order to gain mastery of our other lessons.

The soul—the "core" of a person— is the only thing that survives or matters, my mother realized. Souls exhibit their natures clearly. There were no faces, no bodies, and nothing to hide behind, yet she recognized each for exactly who they were. Their physical facade was no longer a part of them. It was left behind as a remembrance of the role they once played in the lives of their loved ones, to be enshrined in the memory of their existence. This testament to the truth of their former physical being is all that remains here on Earth. Their true essence had transcended.

My mother learned how unimportant our exterior appearance and physical mannerisms actually are, and how shallow our attachment to their value is. Her lesson to learn on that level was to neither judge people by appearance—including race, color, or creed—nor by their financial status or level of education. It was to discover who they really *are,* to see what's inside, to get past the exterior and behold their real identity. And, although this was a lesson she already knew *here,* somehow the illumination gained over *there* was infinitely more expansive.

It was impossible to judge the passage of time. My mother knew that she was up there long enough to rise through all the levels. She also knew that each of the levels taught different lessons.

The first level was that of earthbound souls—those who aren't ready to leave. These are the ones having a difficult time separating themselves from the familiar. They're usually spirits who feel that they have unfinished business to attend to. They may have left sick or disabled loved ones whose care was their responsibility (and they're reluctant to desert them), lingering on this first level until they feel able to release themselves from their earthly bonds. Or, they may have met a rapid or violent death that didn't allow them the time to understand that they had died, as well as the process they would have to go through to follow the path of ascension. Either way, they still feel strong ties to the living and are just not ready to let go. Until they come to the realization that they can no longer function on this plane, that they no longer belong here, and that they are no longer of this dimension, they will remain on the first level—the closest to their former life.

My mother's memories from the second level seem somewhat vague, yet her memories from the third are quite vivid.

When she rose to the third level, she remembers experiencing a heavy feeling. She felt a sadness when she realized that this was the level of those who had taken their own lives. These souls were now in limbo. They seemed to have been isolated, moving neither up nor down. They had no direction. There was an aimless quality to their presence. Would they be allowed to ascend at some point in order to complete their lesson and evolve in their development? She couldn't comprehend that they would not. Maybe it was just taking them longer, but this, she felt, was pure speculation. This was not an answer my mother was able to bring back. Whatever the case, these souls were not at rest—and experiencing this level was very unpleasant, not only for those spending their time there, but for those passing through as well. The lesson from this, the third level, was indelible and clear: *Taking your own life interrupts God's plan.*

There were other lessons my mother was able to bring back as well. She was shown the futility of mourning for those who have died. If there was one regret experienced by the spirits who had passed, it was the pain suffered by those they left behind. They want us to rejoice in their passing, to "trumpet them home," because when we die, we are where we want to be. Our grieving is for *our* loss, the loss of the place in our lives once occupied by that person. Their existence, whether experienced as pleasant or unpleasant, was part of our learning process.

When they die, we lose that lesson's "source." Hopefully, we've either learned what we were to have learned, or, by reflecting upon their life as it intermingled with ours, we would eventually be able to do so. She knew that the passage of time—from when we leave heaven to go through our lives here on Earth to when we return—is but a snap of the fingers in our eternal consciousness, and that we will all be together "momentarily." It is then that we realize that this is how it was meant to be.

She was also shown that, no matter what seemingly terrible or unfair things happen to people here on Earth, it's not God's *fault.* When innocent children are killed, good people die after prolonged illnesses, or someone is injured or disfigured, it has nothing to do with *blame* or *being wrong.* These are *our* lessons to learn—the ones in *our* divine plan—and we've agreed to carry them out. They are lessons for our evolution—for both the givers and the receivers.

In the larger picture, *these occurrences are under the direction and control of the person experiencing them.* Understanding this, she could see how inappropriate it is to question how God could let such things happen, or, based upon these events, to question whether God exists at all. My mother now understood that there was a perfectly logical explanation for it all. It was *so* perfect that she wondered why she hadn't known it all along. And somehow, seeing the whole picture, she realized that everything—*everything*—is as it should be.

My mother also learned that war is a temporary state of barbarism—an ignorant and inept way of settling differences, and at some point, it will no longer exist. These souls find humankind's addiction to warfare not just primitive, but ridiculous—young men being sent out to fight old men's battles for the acquisition of land. One day, humankind will look back on the whole concept and ask, *Why?* When there are enough evolved souls with vast intelligence to solve problems, there will be an end to war altogether.

My mother even found out why people who, to all appearances, had done "horrible" things in life were received without judgment.

Their actions became lessons from which they were to learn, and from which they were to become more perfect beings. They were to evolve from the level of their choices. Of course, they would have to come back to Earth again and again until they absorbed the knowledge derived from the far-reaching consequences of their behavior. They would go through this cycle of birth and rebirth for as long as it took them to evolve and finally return Home.

When the lessons were complete, my mother ascended to the top level. Once there, she stopped rising and began gliding effortlessly forward, drawn steadily and purposefully toward some kind of force. The most beautiful colors and shapes whirled past her on either side. They were like landscapes, except . . . there was no land. Somehow she knew that they were flowers and trees, yet they were in no way like anything here on Earth. These unique, indescribable hues and forms that didn't exist in the world she'd left behind filled her with wonder.

Gradually, my mother became aware that she was skimming above a kind of road, a lane lined on either side by familiar souls—friends, relatives, and people she knew from many lifetimes. They had come to receive her, to guide her and let her know that everything was okay. It was an indescribable feeling of peace and bliss.

At the far end of the road, my mother saw a light. It was like the sun, so bright that she was afraid it would burn her eyes. Surprisingly, even as she drew closer, her eyes felt no pain. The exquisite glow of the light seemed familiar—somehow comfortable. She found herself surrounded by its corona and knew that the light was much more than just a radiance: It was the core of the Supreme Being. She had reached the level of the all-knowing, all-consuming, all-accepting, and all-loving Light. My mother knew she was *Home*. This was where she belonged. This was where she had come from.

Then, the Light communicated with her without words. With a nonverbal thought or two, it conveyed enough information to fill volumes. It spread her lifetime—*this* lifetime—out before her in pictures. She could actually feel the pain or joy she'd given others.

Through this process, she was receiving her lessons—*without any judgment.* However, although there was no judgment, *she* knew it was a good life.

After a while, my mother was given the knowledge that she was being sent back. But she didn't *want* to go. Funny, in spite of all the struggle she'd put up against dying in the first place, she really didn't want to leave at all now. She was so beautifully at peace—ensconced in her new surroundings, her new understandings, her old friends. She wanted to stay for an eternity. How could anyone expect her to leave?

In answer to these silent pleas, my mother was made to understand that she hadn't finished her job back on Earth: She had to return to raise her child. Part of the reason she'd been brought up here was to acquire special insight into how to do just that!

Suddenly, my mother felt herself being drawn out from the core of the Light and back along the path that she'd previously traveled. But now she was going in the opposite direction, and she knew she was returning to her life on Earth. Leaving the familiar souls, the colors and shapes, and the Light Itself, made her feel a deep yearning and sadness.

As she receded from the Light, my mother's knowledge began slipping away. She knew that she'd been *programmed* to forget; she wasn't *supposed* to remember. She tried desperately to cling to what was left, knowing that this was definitely not a dream. She struggled to hang on to the memories and impressions, many of which were gone already, and she felt a terrible loss. However, she felt an inner peace, now armed with the knowledge that when it was her time to return Home, she would be welcomed with love. This, she knew she would remember. She no longer feared death.

At that moment, my mother heard the distant sound of motors. This time they started at the top of her head and began to work their way down. Beyond the roar, she began to hear voices—human voices—and then the beating of her own heart.

Most of the pain, she noticed, was gone.

The motors moved down, down, down . . . their roar fading in intensity. Soon there was nothing left of the motors but a tingling in the soles of her feet. And then not even that. It was over. She had returned to what people like to think of as the "real" world.

A very relieved-looking doctor leaned over her, smiling. "Congratulations, Lois," she said. "You have a beautiful baby boy."

They hadn't shown me to my mother yet. First they had to clean me up, weigh me, and count my toes. So, it was on to her hospital room. As they wheeled my mother into the hallway, the total sense of what she'd experienced and absorbed suddenly overwhelmed her. She intuitively knew that she had already forgotten many of the insights which, only moments ago, were hers: why the sky was blue, why the grass was green, why the world was round, and how creation came about—the perfect logic of it all. Yet she also knew with certainty that there *is* a Supreme Being. There *is* a God.

There was also one realization that she brought back with unequivocal clarity: *We are placed here to learn lessons that make us more complete souls. We have to live this plan out on this level before we're ready to go on to another level. That's why some people are old souls, while others are young ones.*

There was no question that she *had* changed. All of her life she'd been compulsive, a perfectionist, but now my mother decided that it was time to go easier on herself . . . and others. That is, maybe she'd allow a bit of dust inside the house, not carry a bottle of Lysol on vacation trips to wipe down the insides of the hotel bathrooms, and begin to accept things as they are.

As the gurney rolled down the corridor, my father appeared at my mother's side, keeping pace. She gestured for him to bend closer. "When we get back to the room," she whispered, "I have something to tell you that I've been programmed to forget."

When they were in the room together, alone except for a couple of women in hospital beds, my mother whispered, "Don't repeat anything I say, Sonny. People will think I'm crazy."

"I won't."

She went on to describe everything she could still remember, trying to save the few grains of sand that clung to her fingers. My father listened quietly, and she was certain that he didn't doubt a single word she said. He knew she would never make up such a crazy story.

When she was done, exhaustion began to pull her into sleep. She urged my father to go home and write everything down as soon as he could. This information was too precious to lose. He agreed.

She lay back in bed. So many questions. Something very unusual had gone on in that delivery room. She knew it wasn't a dream, if only because dreams don't make you change, not in such a profound way. How could you go into a dream being afraid of death and come out not only feeling unafraid, but actually feeling at ease with it—and knowing that you'd *always* feel that way?!

My mother wanted to delve deeper into her experience. In particular, she wanted to know exactly what had been going on with her body in the delivery room while her consciousness was off communing with beings of pure light.

She soon discovered that finding out wasn't going to be so easy.

When my mother asked the doctor if anything "strange" had happened in the delivery room, she was told, "No, it was a normal delivery." According to the doctor, the only complication, a minor one at that, had been the necessity of using forceps to move the baby into proper birth position—a very common practice at the time.

A normal delivery? This couldn't be the truth. The phrase "normal delivery" didn't coincide with "We're losing her."

Next, my mother questioned the R.N.'s who had worked with her in either the labor or delivery rooms, but she couldn't get anyone to own up to remembering her speaking in tongues, nor admit to any problems at all.

"Everything went just fine," she was told.

If M.D.'s and R.N.'s were the only people present during the birthing process, that would probably have been the end of it. But eventually my mother remembered a practical nurse who had also been in the O.R. during my delivery. Practical nurses worked in the trenches. They went about their business quietly, efficiently, and without fanfare. They often went unnoticed and were almost always underappreciated. *Practical nurses didn't have much reason to hide the truth when things went wrong.*

So my mother confronted the practical nurse, saying, "I know something happened to me in that O.R."

After a long pause, the nurse shrugged. "I can't talk about it, but all I *can* tell you is, *you . . . were . . . lucky.*"

We're losing her?

You were lucky?

This was enough to confirm what my mother already knew: Something special *had* happened to her that day in the delivery room, something that went far beyond the joy of squeezing little me into the world without the benefit of anesthesia. The doctors *had*, in fact, lost her. She had died—and returned. In fact, she would come to think of what happened to her not as a "near-death" experience, but as a "life-after-death" experience. "Near-death" is a watered-down term. My mother hadn't been *near* death. She'd *died*. And like other people who have died and come back, she'd returned a different person. She now understood that whatever came her way in life, "good" or "bad," it would be exactly what her soul needed at that time in order to progress. "You *do* come back . . . until you get it right." It's part of the evolution.

(From *The Reconnection*, Hay House, 2001)

Candace B. Pert, Ph.D.

Michael Ruff

Candace Pert, Ph.D., the author of *Everything You Need to Know to Feel Go(o)d,* is an internationally recognized psychopharmacologist and a former research professor at Georgetown University School of Medicine and section chief at the National Institute of Mental Health. She has published more than 250 scientific articles and has lectured worldwide on pharmacology, neuroanatomy, and her own leading-edge research on emotions and the bodymind connection.

Candace's recent appearance in the film *What the Bleep Do We Know!?* and her 1997 best-selling book, *Molecules of Emotion: The Science Behind Mind-Body Medicine,* have popularized her groundbreaking theories on consciousness, neuropeptides, and reality.

Website: **www.candacepert.com**

WHEN YOU FEEL,
YOU HEAL

The turning point in my own spiritual evolution, as well as my development as a scientist, occurred in 1985 at a scientific symposium on AIDS, on the island of Maui, Hawaii. It was there that I heard and followed the voice of God, an inner guidance that set my mission and life's purpose for the next 20 years and continues to inform the thrust of my research today.

In 1997, my first book, *Molecules of Emotion,* described how I'd developed my theory of emotions; and how my husband, Dr. Michael Ruff, and I brought forth an interdisciplinary revolution showing the ways that the body and mind are inextricably linked as one entity. But the real reason that I wrote the book was to tell the story of our joint invention—a nontoxic, highly potent drug for use in the treatment of AIDS, called Peptide T.

The actual conception of Peptide T occurred after Michael and I had hiked to the summit of Haleakala Crater on Maui and then spoke at the American College of Neuropsychopharmacology's first world symposium on neuroAIDS. The year was 1985, and neuroAIDS was the newly recognized condition in which the HIV virus affected brain functioning.

Coming off the hiking trail and arriving back down at sea level, Michael and I were elated from the strenuous-but-inspiring, endorphin-pumping adventure and eager to attend the conference. We had much good data to present about the brain and immune system sharing a common cellular receptor—a tiny structure on the surface of cells—called the CD4 receptor. At the time, this was thought to be the only entry point into the cell for the infection of HIV, and finding it on brain, as well as immune cells, had all kinds of very exciting implications for finding a treatment.

We sat in the audience, still in an altered state from the 12-mile round-trip, 8,000-foot climb and hike through the crater, and listened carefully to what others were presenting about the new disease known as AIDS. Up until that time, the condition had been somewhat abstract to me. Scientists in the infectious-disease department of our research world, the National Institutes of Health, were working on it, but AIDS wasn't something that those of us in mental health had paid much attention to.

The last presenter to speak before me, a woman psychologist, showed slides of her patients ravaged from the disease—mostly artists, musicians, and sensitive-looking men from the gay communities of San Francisco; Provincetown, Massachusetts; and New York City. As I watched, I had a chance to study the gaunt, terrified faces of these suffering human beings. I felt my heart open with compassion for their plight, and I was so moved by the intensity of their condition that my eyes filled with tears and I had to choke back sobs. These days, I cry for the women, children, villages, societies, and nations that bear the brunt of the current pandemic.

Finally, it was my turn to lecture. I stood up and walked slowly to the podium to begin my talk. I was alert and emotionally open as I clicked through my slides, describing the hard data. It was toward the end of my presentation, when I was showing a visual of how CD4 receptors were distributed in the brain, that I heard unplanned words coming out of my mouth.

"Here we have what looks like a typical peptide-receptor pattern," I began, pointing to the pattern of receptors where the virus was connecting. But then I shocked myself by saying, "If we could find the natural, bodily peptide that fits into this CD4 receptor and blocks the entry of the virus, we could manufacture this peptide and produce a drug that would be effective and nontoxic to treat AIDS."

I was so surprised to hear my own words that I paused, and in the gap, I heard a voice—one that was loud and booming—coming from inside my head and commanding me: *And you should do that!*

Was it the voice of God that spoke to me? Maybe it was my subconscious mind, or the archetypal unconscious, or a spiritual higher consciousness—I didn't know! I could only be certain that I'd been given my marching orders to find the body's own peptide, one that would fit a receptor to inhibit entry of the virus, and then create a drug from it in the lab. I was immediately electrified by the possibility of a receptor-based treatment for AIDS, one that would be totally natural, an imitation of the body's own internal chemical!

The very next morning, I was on the phone from Hawaii to my lab back in Maryland, setting up a computer-assisted database search for our entry-blocking peptide. At the time, scientists had cracked the complete sequence of over 5,000 amino acids for the part of the HIV virus that sticks into the receptor to gain entry. Now all we needed to do was search the sequenced peptides in the body for a match.

We found it right off. The matching peptide was only eight amino acids long, making it short and easy to manufacture. We did an experiment to show how our lab-made version of the body's own chemical worked; and in 1986, we published our very positive results in *Proceedings of the National Academy of Sciences,* one of the scientific establishment's most prestigious—and difficult to get into—journals. What we'd found was a mimetic (or "imitation") of the body's own neuropeptide hormone, a natural, nontoxic, highly potent, antiviral treatment for AIDS that we named after the amino acid that composed four of the eight in the chain, Threonine, or Peptide T. . . .

The funding for Peptide T eventually came—albeit slowly and painfully, and my husband I created a foundation to raise the funds ourselves. Today, our drug has been tested in several clinical trials with positive results and published data showing that Peptide T is highly promising to effectively treat, and possibly even cure, HIV disease because of the things that it does. Two important effects are lowering the level of the virus in human blood plasma and flushing the cellular reservoirs where the virus hides, waiting to emerge and reinfect new cells.

The discovery of Peptide T was a turning point for me in embracing the power of consciousness to manifest miracles and bring about unpredictable futures, and it has been a humbling journey. It wasn't my idea to go looking for this premature discovery— I was simply following directions!

But I did allow myself to be moved by compassion for people suffering from AIDS, and that was the key to me hearing my own inner voice. I've said that emotions are a bridge that links the spiritual to the material world, and the discovery of Peptide T clearly demonstrates the truth of that statement. When our hearts are open and our feelings are flowing as they're designed to do, we're all vulnerable to the divine. In the case of my discovery, compassion opened the door for me to literally see and hear the way to bring an end to the disease.

In other words, when we feel, we heal. The word *heal* has a common origin with the words *whole* and *holy,* pointing to a relationship of body to spirit. All emotions bring us closer to our true nature and powerful creative capacity, whether we call it "consciousness" or "God." How our biochemicals of emotion make this possible, the very physiology of the bodymind, is the science that underlies feeling good and feeling God.

(From *Everything You Need to Know to Feel Go(o)d,* Hay House, 2006)

John Randolph Price

Images, 1999

John Randolph Price is an internationally known, award-winning author and lecturer. Formerly a CEO in the corporate world, he has devoted over a quarter of a century to researching the mysteries of ancient wisdom and incorporating those findings into the writing of many books, including *The Abundance Book, Practical Spirituality,* and *Nothing Is Too Good to Be True.*

In 1981, John and his wife, Jan, formed the Quartus Foundation, a spiritual research organization headquartered in the Texas hill country town of Boerne, near San Antonio, where they live with their two springer spaniels, Maggi and Casey.

Website: **www.quartus.org**

OUR BABY
IS BACK!

This story begins on the evening of July 17, 1981. My wife, Jan, and I had finished dinner and were watching a movie on TV. It wasn't a sad show, but suddenly tears started rolling down my cheeks, and my heart became so heavy that I had to get up and go outside. Jan knew something was wrong but said nothing, knowing that when I was ready to talk about it, I would. I sat down on the grass in the backyard beside our dog Brandy—a ten-year-old springer spaniel who was as much a part of our lives as our very own children.

For more than an hour, I sat there and bawled like a baby, with a sadness unlike anything I'd ever experienced. When I finally went back into the house, I really had nothing to tell Jan, because I had no idea why I'd been so grief stricken. It wasn't until the next morning that I knew.

While we were having breakfast that next day, Brandy was on the floor between us—and we both noticed that she was having difficulty breathing. She'd been sick off and on for about three months, and we'd taken her to the vet several times for various medications. And, of course, we'd worked with her spiritually; but in looking back, this kind of treatment was done much too casually. Anyway, we picked her up and drove to the vet as quickly as possible, but within minutes of getting there, she died.

Then I knew what I'd been "told" the night before—and the grief came back like a tidal wave, engulfing both of us. Oh, how we cried! And the tears flowed for the rest of the day and into the night . . . and the next morning, there was still no relief.

During meditation on Sunday, which I found extremely difficult to get into, something quite unexpected happened. All of a sudden, Brandy appeared right in front of me, saying, "Lift up your vision." I was startled—and the first thought that came into my mind was, *Don't judge by appearances.*

Then, two nights later, I had a dream. I could see Brandy through a thin curtain. I was on one side, and she was on the other, and she was trying desperately to claw her way through. I woke up, shook Jan, and told her that we must release Brandy at once . . . that our grief was holding her back from her highest good. So we spoke the word to let her go, and with very wet eyes went back to sleep.

A week later, an unusual sequence of dreams began—each about a week apart. In the first one, I was walking down a country road, and Brandy came running up beside me, saying, "Tell Mommy I'm coming back." And I said (for some strange reason), "That's not her name; her name is Jan." Brandy replied: "But you always called her Mommy in front of me." Then she ran off down the road. I didn't say anything to Jan the next morning. After all, it was only a dream.

In the second dream, I was walking down that same country road, and here comes Brandy again, almost hollering this time: "You didn't tell Mommy that I'm coming back." I just smiled at her, and she said again, "You'd better tell her, because I'm coming back on October 20th."

Well, you can imagine what happened when the alarm went off the next morning. I said, "Jan, I've got something to tell you . . . something a bit strange, but I've been told that I'd *better* tell you." Then I reviewed both dreams. Jan just looked at me with her big brown eyes and didn't say anything.

Then about a week later, I had the third dream. This time I was leaning against a fence talking to Brandy (can't remember that particular conversation), and another springer spaniel runs up. I lean down to pat her, and Brandy says, "Be careful; she's four years old."

And I asked, "What does that mean?"

She replied, with a big grin on her face, "You'll know."

In the next dream, we were walking down that country road again, talking like two old friends. (She was walking upright and was as tall as I was.) She said, "By the way, I'm changing my consciousness this time."

I stopped, looked right in her eyes, and asked, "But why? I love you the way you are!"

She responded, "Oh, I'll still be the same dog, the same soul, but I don't want to have another heart attack, so I'm changing my consciousness."

I said, "I understand."

In dream number five, she tells me to "look for the white!" And when I ask what that means, she just grins and says, "You'll know." And in the final dream, she's very emphatic in saying, "Don't try to find me. Don't do anything. It's all been worked out, so don't run around looking for me. You'll know!"

In September, our daughter, Susan, moved from Houston to Austin, bringing her huge cat with her, and moved in with us until she could find her own apartment. When she arrived, Jan noticed a deep scratch on the cat and suggested that "Puff" be taken to the vet. While she and Susan were there, the vet asked, "Jan, are you and John ready for another dog yet?"

Jan, being very cautious, said, "I don't know . . . we'll just wait and see."

And the vet said, "Well, if you decide you want another springer, here's the name and telephone number of a woman whose dog is going to have a litter."

Jan took the information and called the woman that night. After checking us out in what seemed like an FBI investigation, Jan was finally able to ask, "When are the pups due?"

The woman answered, "October 20th." We got goose bumps.

The woman then said, "And this is my springer's first litter."

Jan asked, "How old is your dog?"

The reply: "Four years old."

We were right on target at this point, but we couldn't do anything else until the pups were born. ("Look for the white!" Brandy had said.) But just as soon as we heard that the baby springers had arrived, Jan and I were kneeling over the box . . . and right in the middle of the litter was a little female with huge white patches over a background of liver-brown. (Brandy had been almost all brown.) We immediately put in our claim for *that* one, and visited her constantly until we could bring her home.

Brandy always had an unusual way of greeting us. She would sit down on her haunches and raise her two front paws in the air—in almost a "Take me, I'm yours" kind of posture. When the new pups were four weeks old, we visited them on a Sunday afternoon, and they were all out playing in the grass. As we got out of the car and walked across the lawn, the little white-and-brown one turned, saw us coming, managed to get up on her little rear end, and held her paws up high—just like Brandy used to do. This almost did Jan in, and she ran across the yard squealing, "My baby, my baby!"

When we brought her home at six weeks, she telepathically told us that she wanted a new name (we had considered calling her Brandy again). So after discussing various names, she decided on "Magnificent Brandy, Too"—and we called her Maggi for short. And yes, she had that same gentle, loving, joy-filled personality that she displayed before. In the more than 12 years she was with us, she continued to teach us so much . . . including a special reverence for all life, and the Truth that a soul never dies . . . not even a dog's . . . *especially* not a dog's!

(From *Practical Spirituality,* Hay House, 1985, 1996)

Carol Ritberger, Ph.D.

Jennifer Wu Photography

Carol Ritberger, Ph.D., the author of *What Color Is Your Personality?* and *Your Personality, Your Health,* among other works, is a medical intuitive and an innovative leader in the field of personality typology. Her work has been featured on television, radio, and in numerous national magazines.

Carol lives in Northern California, with her husband, Bruce, with whom she cofounded The Ritberger Institute, which offers personal and professional development programs.

Website: **www.ritberger.com**

A Different
Set of Eyes

As I look back on the events that altered the way I now live my life and "see" the world, I am still in awe at the synchronicity of events. Things happen when you're ready to accept them even though you may not be consciously aware of their impact on your life. What I am going to tell you is a story of how my world was turned inside out by a series of bizarre events that changed my sight and my life forever.

Early in 1981, I was between consulting contracts, so a friend asked me if I would like to help out in her booth at a health and beauty show. The second day of the event, I was walking the show floor looking at the displays, at the same time responding to a gut feeling that maybe there was an opportunity waiting to present itself. As I wandered around, a hand grabbed me by the shoulder from behind. I turned around and saw a small, delicate woman pulling at me. She said that she must talk to me. She had something important to tell me and she wanted to read my palm. I politely told her, "No, thank you, I don't believe in that stuff."

Later in the day, I felt a hand on my shoulder and heard that now-familiar voice saying that she must talk with me. I turned around and heatedly said, "Leave me alone! I don't believe in what you do, and I don't want to talk to you. Go away." She persisted and volunteered that I was going to have three brushes with death in a two-week period of time, and that the third time I would have to choose whether I would go or stay.

The woman quickly left after giving me her message. For several minutes I simply stood there asking myself, *Now what?* Part of my education is in the field of behavioral psychology, so I'm familiar with the perspective that states that an emotionally charged thought, once planted in the conscious mind, may become a reality.

Finally, after analyzing what had happened, I decided to dismiss the whole thing. I convinced myself that the woman didn't know what she was talking about.

The next day I asked my mother to go to the show with me, and after a long day that went well into the night, we were finally on our way home in my car. It was late, and I was both physically and emotionally drained. In that half-conscious state, I looked in the rearview mirror and saw all four lanes of the freeway filled with headlights that were fast approaching us. I turned to my mother and said that I had a very bad feeling that there was going to be a terrible accident. What seemed like only seconds later, there was a 16-car pileup, and six teenagers were killed. As we waited for the emergency vehicles to arrive, my mother turned to me and said, "Carol, do you think that woman at the show was right, and this could have been number one?"

The second event took place the following week. I was having lunch with a very good friend. We talked about what was going on in our lives, and I told her about the strange experience that had happened the week before. She became very upset with me and my unwillingness to accept the warning the woman had given me.

I left the restaurant extremely agitated and couldn't understand why my friend had become so antagonistic and angry. Distracted by the events, I put my purse on top of my car to unlock the door. After getting on the freeway, I saw something blow off the top of my car. Instantly I remembered my purse. I pulled over to the side of the road and backed up to see if it was possible to retrieve it. After checking the freeway, it appeared that I had plenty of time to run out and pick up my purse and the contents that spilled out. The purse landed in the middle lane. I ran out to pick it up.

As I kneeled down, I heard the frightening sound of a diesel horn. When I looked up, I saw an 18-wheeler in my lane.

The next few seconds passed as if I were watching in slow motion. The truck swerved to miss me, and its trailer hit the center divider. The wind pressure was so great that it knocked me flat against the pavement. All traffic came to a halt. I lay there thinking, *Hooray, I am not dead. Crazy, maybe, but not dead.*

For the next few days, I stayed home. I was afraid to get in the car and certainly wanted nothing to do with freeways. All I could wonder about was what number three would be like after the first two incidents. I was obsessed with fear and the thought of dying.

Now, I believe that there is much we can learn about ourselves in times of emotional turmoil. The lesson from the events that had taken place was that it forced me to reprioritize what was important and reevaluate my beliefs surrounding life and death. I had many in-depth conversations with God to try to help me to understand. I was full of questions that for the first time in my life neither my education nor my logical mind could answer. I felt I was trying to understand at a different level—one that was vague, yet reassuring and comforting in its message. There was great peace within me from that new thinking,

Finally, I decided that enough was enough. I couldn't stay home the rest of my life trying to avoid a third incident. That evening I joined my mother and some friends for dinner at a restaurant. As we sat enjoying the food, I began to choke and had difficulty breathing. Everyone asked if I was okay, and I said yes, I just needed some fresh air. I went outside, and when I returned, I again began to have trouble breathing. This time I couldn't get a full breath. I panicked and got up to leave. When I did, I must have fainted, although I felt fully conscious. Instead of going to the hospital, I opted to go home. About two o'clock in the morning, I woke up fully drenched in sweat. I was burning up. Again, I couldn't breathe. I called to my mother to help me. All I remember saying is, "Mom, pray with me; I think I'm dying."

I can't tell you exactly where I went for the next 18 hours, but I remember watching people work on me trying to get me to breathe. I found myself above my body, looking at it with a sense of wonderment. As I seemed to float there, I turned to see what appeared to be bright lights moving toward me. As the lights got closer, I could make out shapes within them. I knew that I recognized them. At one point, I asked them if I was dead. I was told yes, but I could still make a choice. Here was that choice thing. If I were dead, then what choice was there?

I loved where I was. I felt free and light. There was no heaviness of being attached to my body, and I wanted to savor every feeling. There was a tremendous sense of joy and no fear. I was full of questions for my newfound light friends. I remember being told that while I was good at asking questions, I needed to listen to the answers. My opinions and expectations of life, myself, and others were coloring my perspective. They were inhibiting my ability to move forward and to do what I'd chosen to do.

Suddenly, like a splash of cold water, I was jolted back to reality. I heard my daughter run into my room and call to me, "Mom, I need you to come play with me!" I felt myself falling. When I opened my eyes, all I could see were bright, blinding lights. The room was full of colors. It appeared that everyone in the room had a glow about them, just like my light friends. Was this reaction due to the drugs I'd been given or the trauma to my body? The only explanation offered was that I may have suffered some temporary vision damage because of loss of oxygen to the brain.

I began noticing how the colors within the glow changed from person to person. Some people were more colorful; some people's lights stayed close to them; others extended out several feet. I became aware that while each person's lights and colors seemed different, they each had some similarities. Their glow seemed to pulsate depending on what they were saying and how emotional they were. And, the colors I saw in each person were all pretty much the same basic hues.

One morning as I was lying in bed, I got a flash of insight and realized that my choice must have been to come back and learn how to see life through a different set of eyes. Somehow my sight was changed. And, curiously enough, although I could see lights around others, I couldn't see them around myself.

Two weeks after getting back on my feet, I had to fly from California to Colorado on business. I wasn't sure how I was going to do since my eyesight hadn't returned to normal. The lights were so irritating and bright that I needed to wear sunglasses most of the time. As I sat there trying to look inconspicuous, I noticed that the lights surrounding a young girl sitting near me were different from those I'd seen around others. This girl's lights had holes in them—holes with no light. Her colors were muted, gray, and dark. Her lights looked like the flame of a candle struggling to stay lit. I hoped that she wasn't getting on my flight.

I was getting aboard when I looked up to see a woman and the young girl coming down the aisle toward me. I immediately looked away, hoping that they wouldn't stop and sit by me, but the woman asked if they could sit next to me since their seats were next to the exit door. What could I say? A short time into the flight, the woman started talking to me. She told me that they were going to Colorado to see a specialist for her daughter. She said her daughter had a serious blood disease, and this specialist was their last hope.

Just before we landed, the woman thanked me for listening and said that she wanted to keep in touch to tell me the results of their visit. Reluctantly, I gave her a business card. Three weeks later, I received a letter from her saying that her daughter had died. This was my first wake-up call telling me that I needed to find out more about what all of these lights and colors meant and why they weren't the same in every person.

For the next year and a half, I spent time seeing psychologists, psychiatrists, optometrists, and ophthalmologists trying to find answers. Why did my sight not return to normal? Finally, a psychologist I had once seen called to ask me if I'd ever heard of the human aura or of Edgar Cayce. I answered no to both of her questions. She then strongly encouraged me to read all I could about both. That same day, I went out and bought every book I could find about those two subjects. I look back now and thank the universe for this highly intuitive lady who finally helped me embark on my journey toward understanding. Another coincidence? I don't think so.

After a while, I did start to notice that my sight was changing.

Instead of seeing a mist of light around people, the lights and colors were becoming more defined, with the colors focusing on different areas of the body. When people were angry or stressed, it showed in specific areas of their bodies. People who were happy and optimistic had an overall glow about them. Their colors were different and bright, and their lights reached out several feet from their bodies.

At the same time I was exploring my newfound capabilities, I was continuing my education in the psychology of personality behavior. It was not that I didn't enjoy what I could do or how it seemed to help others. It was just that my logical mind was having a difficult time dealing with it and accepting what was happening. Deep down inside, I began to understand that there was a connection between the human aura, colors, chakras, and personality characteristics. My research and quest for understanding kept indicating that all of these factors play an important role in why people act the way they do, why they create the illnesses they do, why stress to one person is a stimulus to another, and why stress seemed to be a significant contributor to dysfunction.

It was six years into my journey when one morning I looked in the mirror and I saw lights around me. My overall light was weak, and it had spots within it that were bright red. Some areas of my body hardly contained any light at all.

What I came to understand was that I wasn't dying. Rather, I was being shown something to help me learn. My own aura was showing me where there were imbalances in my body—that is, where I hadn't been taking care of myself. It was showing me that all of the stress from the events over the past several years was affecting my body negatively. This created a higher awareness within me—one that I needed to share. That awareness was that while it may be easier to give to others, caretaking must begin with ourselves if we're to have the capacity to truly nurture others.

(From *Your Personality, Your Health*, Hay House, 1998)

Ron Roth, Ph.D.

Portraits by Anthony

Ron Roth, Ph.D., is an internationally known teacher, spiritual healer, and modern-day mystic. He has appeared on many TV and radio programs and is the author of several books, including *The Healing Path of Prayer*, *Holy Spirit*, and *Prayer and the Five Stages of Healing* (with Peter Occhiogrosso). He served in the Roman Catholic priesthood for more than 25 years and is the founder of Celebrating Life Institutes in Peru, Illinois, where he lives.

Website: **www.ronroth.com**

AND I
FORGIVE *YOU!*

When my father had his first brush with death, I was shocked at the sight. I went into his room and saw him bleeding from the nose and the mouth, with blood all over the walls. My father was an alcoholic, and his liver was starting to give out. None of us knew what to do. My first reaction was to think, *I'm going to pray. God, if this is his time to go, then let him go in peace now. If not, heal him now.*

He was healed instantly, and I thought, *This is great!*

The only problem was that he gave up drinking for about six months and then went back to it. So the next time he had an attack like that, it really *was* time to go, because his liver had disintegrated. In the hospital, you could even see bits of his liver coming through the tube, and he was in a state of what I called "coma vibration." He was in a coma, but his body was shaking up and down without stopping. The doctors tried everything to stop the shaking, but to no avail. I asked if he was conscious, and they said he wasn't. This was before the case studies had come out demonstrating that unconscious patients who were being operated on could hear everything the doctors were saying, yet I intuitively knew this. I said to God that there must be something I could do to stop the awful shaking. And I heard an inner voice telling me, *"Yes, just tell it to stop."*

I did, very softly but firmly, and that was the end of it. The shaking stopped. As I sat there, I heard the voice say to me, *"Now, forgive your father."* At first I thought it was the "devil" this time. All I could think was that my father was a bad man who drank too much and yelled at us and made everyone unhappy. How could I forgive him for that? The voice came again: *"Forgive him."* Finally I surrendered to it. I stood up over the bed and actually whispered aloud, "Dad, I forgive you."

Immediately, he opened his eyes and looked at me. "And I forgive you," he said. Then he closed his eyes and seemed to return to his coma. I was stunned. My first reaction was, *Oh my God, that's wonderful.* And then I thought, *What do you mean, you forgive me?*

It was close to midnight, and my mother and I were both in the room. Then with all the windows in the hospital closed, we could smell a fragrant aroma of flowers wafting through the room. I went out into the hallway to see who was bringing in flowers. I opened the windows to see if it was coming from outside, but when I stuck my head out, I couldn't smell anything.

My mother said it was time to go. We lived only ten minutes away, yet I knew that by the time we got home, my father would be dead. When we arrived home, the phone was already ringing. It was the nurse telling us to come back because Dad had passed away just after we left. I felt no resentment, however, because I'd had the opportunity for closure. And I was able to reach closure only because I listened to the voice that was telling me, in essence, to surrender by letting go of my bitterness toward my father for being an alcoholic. I don't know where I would have gone psychically or what my life would be right now without having had the chance to forgive him.

If you've never had the opportunity to put closure on something, you can still do it in the world of spirit. You can still go back to that time by setting the scene again in your mind. If it's someone you never forgave for hurting you, you can go back and do the forgiving and let them forgive you. Remember that none of us is completely guiltless; we've all done things to each other that we need to heal emotionally.

Physical healing isn't the only kind . . . the Spirit of God is very good at emotional healing, too!

(From *Holy Spirit for Healing,* Hay House, 2001)

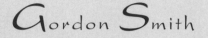

Gordon Smith

Mark Guthrie

Gordon Smith, the author of *Spirit Messenger* and *The Unbelievable Truth,* is an astoundingly accurate medium from Glasgow, Scotland, who's renowned for his ability to give exact names of people, places, and even streets. Gordon travels all around the world demonstrating his abilities, offering healing and comfort to thousands of people. His extraordinary skills have attracted the attention of university scientists researching psychic phenomena, as well as countless numbers of journalists and documentary producers.

Website: **www.psychicbarber.com**

A Few Slips
of the Tongue

Please don't get me wrong. I don't make fun of mediums or Spiritualism, especially when true and sincere practitioners are helping many individuals who really do need support at difficult times in their lives. But humorous situations sometimes arise when people are trying desperately to be serious.

Albert Best was an extraordinary medium (and a mentor of mine), and one of his greatest features was his ability to laugh, both at himself as well as at some of the ridiculous situations he found himself in. Albert told me the following story:

He had just sat down after demonstrating his unique gift of clairvoyance to a packed London church when his very gracious hostess arose to thank him, and to inform the congregation that Albert would be available for private readings the following day. But whatever the hostess had intended, what she actually said was, "Ladies and gentlemen, I'm sure you will all join with me in thanking Mr. Best for his excellent demonstration of mediumship. Furthermore, I take great delight in announcing that Albert will be holding his privates for three hours tomorrow morning. If anyone would like to book a session with him, please see me at the close of the service."

Albert told me he had a vision of himself cupping his "privates" and charging ten pounds for half-hour sessions! What made this even funnier was that at no time did the hostess realize her mistake, much to the delight of all assembled.

Another slip of the tongue that caused hilarity among a group of Spiritualists occurred in our development circle on a Thursday night. At the end of a circle, the leader would ask each person if they had a message for anyone else in the group. On this particular evening, one lady got to her feet and approached the gentleman who was sitting opposite her, who was wearing a very obvious hairpiece. When our would-be medium began to give him a message, it was apparent that she couldn't take her eyes off his thick black head adornment.

"When I looked at you," she said, "I was aware of North American Indians dancing around you." Still looking at the wig, she added, "Then there was a great scene of the whole tribe."

"The whole tribe," the man repeated rather doubtfully.

"Yes," she replied. "They were dancing around a toupee."

Everybody in the room tried to muffle their laughter, hoping not to embarrass the poor man. As quick as a flash, he came back with a clever reply that gave him the last laugh, saying, "I think, my dear, that the word you are looking for is *tepee*. But thank you for your message. The Indian you saw must be the one who scalped me."

The entire room erupted with laughter, as you can imagine. Some of the funniest things in life seem to happen out of embarrassing situations, although to be honest, I don't know who was the most embarrassed in the end!

(From *Spirit Messenger,* Hay House, 2004)

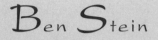

Ben Stein

Greg Bertolini

Ben Stein, the author of *How to Ruin Your Life, The Gift of Peace,* and a number of books on finance (with co-author Phil DeMuth), is a lawyer, economist, writer, actor, teacher, and former game-show host (his show *Win Ben Stein's Money* won seven Emmys). He lives in Southern California with his wife, Alexandra; his son, Thomas; and many dogs and cats. He is very active in fund-raising for animal- and children's-rights charities in Los Angeles and throughout the country.

Website: **www.benstein.com**

THE HOUSE
MY FATHER BUILT

Long ago, maybe in 1960 when he was running against Richard Nixon for President, John F. Kennedy was asked about some unsavory aspects of his father's life. "We all have fathers," he said, meaning that we can't be responsible for what our fathers are. But some of us have fathers whose lives are so honorable that we wish we *could* be identified with what they are. That's how I felt about my father, Herbert Stein, who passed away on September 8, 1999.

My father was winning things from the day he was born: declamation contests, math contests—you name it. When he was 15, he went off to Williams College, and I think you can understand some of the main strengths of my father's makeup from three facts of his college life. First, he had a job at Williams washing dishes at a fraternity that did not admit Jews. Yet he didn't feel at all slighted and didn't recall it bitterly; instead, he was grateful he had work to pay his way through school. Gratitude for what he had, not idle complaining and troublemaking, was one of his life's foundations.

Second, my father tried to find a job every summer that he was at Williams, and in all that time he could only find one day's work. This he *did* recall with some distress, and it also explained something about his compassionate approach to public policy. He had superb analytical ability, but he also knew that analytical ability without compassion is meager and unsatisfactory.

Third, he had the happiest day of his life just falling asleep listening to a famous game in the 1931 World Series on the radio.

This showed his ability to find peace of mind through the broadcast media. They didn't have *Murder, She Wrote* in those days or my father might not have finished college. (You can't imagine how much time he spent watching TV, especially sports.)

His work career since those summers during the Great Depression got much better. I often wish that *his* father could have seen how he turned out. My grandfather used to go to brokerages during the Depression to watch stocks move on the ticker for amusement, even though he had none. What would he have made of a son who, when he was chairman of the President's Council of Economic Advisors, could move markets with what he said? How proud he would have been—and how happy with what my pal Aram rightly calls the greatest miracle of man's existence: America.

My father was modest to the extreme. Whenever I told him how amazed I was at what he made of his life, he always said that this told more about America than about him. He never, in all the time I knew him, ever suggested any way of cutting corners or doing anything even remotely questionable. There was no amount of money that could make him say anything he didn't believe in. I never heard him make a racist remark—which I can also say about my mother and sister. I never saw him make a sexist remark. And I never saw him even look at another woman besides my mother.

Whenever a colleague questioned my father's approach to an issue, his first inquiry was always whether he, my father, might be wrong, not the other guy. When he disagreed, he did it with minimal force and maximum politesse. I never asked him for help of any kind (it's usually some arcane statistic), that he didn't furnish without a murmur, often enthusiastically. His loyalty to his friends was absolute.

But even these things don't really show who my father was. You had to see him at home to know that. You had to see him cheerfully washing dishes after dinner and singing "Drink a Highball at Nightfall" to my mother. You had to see him hold my mother's hand as they watched *Jeopardy!* night after night. After almost 60 years together, my parents were basically one person. They had a level of devotion to one another that is almost unimaginable in my generation.

The House My Father Built

You had to see my father making pancakes from scratch on a 40-year-old frying pan that his mother gave him, feeding my mother, my son, and me and explaining what Washington was like before the war, when there were streetcars. You had to see him in his apartment, puttering around with snacks, making some wise observation about the election, telling jokes, singing songs from his college days, or talking with tears in his eyes about friends.

Richard Nixon, the Stein family's favorite President, began his memoirs by saying, "I was born in a house my father built." In many ways, I still live in a house my father built. It's a great house, filled with books and thought and love, and I feel very lucky to occupy it. And I hope to pass it on to my son.

(From the anthology *In Real Life,* by Karl Zinsmeister, with Karina Rollins, New Beginnings Press/Hay House, 2005)

Caroline Sutherland

N. J. Pelman

Caroline Sutherland, the author of *The Body "Knows": How to Tune In to Your Body and Improve Your Health,* has a vast clinical background as an allergy-testing technician in environmental medicine, where her intuitive gift developed. She was raised in a medical family: Her mother was a dietitian, and both her father and grandfather were medical doctors. As a child, the blueprint of her family lineage created important seeds for her future career as a medical intuitive.

For the past 23 years, she has lectured internationally on the subject, and her intuitive impressions have positively affected the lives of more than 100,000 people. Caroline is the founder of Sutherland Communications, Inc., which offers medical-intuitive training programs, weight-loss programs, and consultation services for adults and children. She is a frequent guest on radio and television.

Website: **www.carolinesutherland.com**

BREAKING THROUGH AND SEEING BEYOND

The gift of medical intuition came to me quite suddenly in the early 1980s when I was working as a physician's assistant and allergy-testing technician for a very busy medical doctor who specialized in environmental medicine. Environmental medicine deals with the human body in relationship to the environment—everything a person eats, breathes, and comes in contact with—and the effect each of these elements has on a person's body. This is the fascinating field in which I was immersed.

After using highly specialized allergy-testing equipment for about a year, I began to hear a very distinct inner voice guiding me to investigate particular areas of the body and examine specific substances—which hadn't been ordered on the test forms. I shared the information that I was "hearing" with the physician I was working for. Fortunately, because he was a very open-minded individual, he agreed to evaluate its validity. Over the ensuing months, we arrived at a place where both of us were working as an incredible team—I intuited each patient's needs more deeply than we were able to do with the diagnostic equipment, and he used his medical knowledge in evaluation and treatment. In a very short time, people were getting well, and the clinic had a year-long waiting list.

This partnership continued for several years, and then I had a strong instinct to leave the clinic and open my own office. I went on to create guided-imagery audiotapes for children and adults, for which I am now rather well known. After a few years in business for myself, I was asked by a naturopathic physician to join his clinic as an allergy-testing technician. He was aware of my intuitive abilities and gratefully accepted my instinctive impressions regarding his patients. In no time, his practice was thriving.

My medical intuitive ability is very specific to the *physical* body. After nearly two decades in environmental medicine, I see the body from that perspective. To help a person, I don't have to be in their actual physical presence—in fact, all I need to know is their name and a little about them, hear their voice, or see their photograph. The minute I connect with the person seeking my help, a flood of data comes to me. The information is very specific. I can intuit foods that a person is allergic/sensitive to, perceive the main systems that may be compromised, observe the state of the gastrointestinal tract or immune system, and check for hormone imbalances or weight problems. I then look at the underlying causes of these problems, when they began, and what may have precipitated them. I also make suggestions regarding their diet, which supplements or botanicals they might benefit from, and so on.

Other useful information is also given to me, such as the length of time for a patient's recovery, whether or not that patient will be compliant, or if indeed they are likely to recover at all. In this nearly 20-year period, I've had the privilege of being part of the assessment and treatment of more than 60,000 people.

I've often thought that my specific medical orientation came to me via my deceased doctor father. He died when I was 26 years old, and our relationship had never been close. Over the years, I believe that "through the veil," or from the other side, he tried to make contact with me on a number of occasions. But, because of my feelings toward him, I pushed this connection away. Years later, after much introspection and deep meditative work, I accepted the nature of our relationship on a karmic level. It was necessary for the development of my potential, and I forgave him. At that moment, I was catapulted into his world—the world of medicine.

In 1983, I went for my yearly physical. I was 38 years old. I was seeing a new doctor, but there was no reason to suspect that this annual checkup would be different from any other one. Although it was difficult to put my finger on the problem, I hadn't been feeling terrific at the time. I'd been having some peculiar symptoms that had me worried, such as numbness and tingling in my arms and hands, mini-blackouts, memory loss, periods of depression, and frequent states of fear and anxiety.

As I lay on the examining table, I decided to come clean and tell this doctor everything I'd been experiencing. After I related my worrisome signs, I went on to tell the doctor of my greatest fear: I'd been bumping into things, and I seemed to be losing my balance or my sense of perception.

After relating this bizarre history, I was expecting the usual knowing look of condescension I'd seen over the years from other doctors. Surprise! *This* doctor responded with interest and compassion and appeared to have an immediate understanding of the problem. After examining me thoroughly, she said that she suspected that allergies to certain foods and a sensitivity to yeast were the culprits.

She suggested that a specific kind of allergist—a specialist in environmental medicine—could help. She then referred me to a doctor colleague of hers who specialized in the treatment of food allergies, the *candida* yeast syndrome, and environmental illness. It was worth investigating. I look back on that day now and give thanks to this forward-thinking physician who changed the course of my life.

Feeling bloated and depressed, I entered the environmental medical clinic. How could this doctor, I thought skeptically, have an answer to such a host of problems?

The next day, during several hours of testing, I was to learn more about the effects of food and chemicals on the body. The kind of testing I was subjected to is called intradermal testing, and it involves the injection of a concentrated amount of each allergen or substance under the skin, at ten-minute intervals. The patient's pulse rate is taken, reactions noted, and a wheal or bump at the injection site is measured.

In my case, milk brought on stomach cramps, postnasal drip, and a dry cough—obviously the "healthy" cottage cheese salad that I ate every day for lunch was doing me no good. Wheat induced a fuzzy head and exhaustion; I could hardly keep my eyes open during the test.

The testing continued. Oranges gave me a pounding sinus headache and pulsating temples. What would I do without my morning O.J.? I experienced fatigue, pain in my hands, and a raised pulse when exposed to chicken. Potatoes caused fatigue and pain in my wrists, hands, and knees. One by one, the basic foods were being crossed off my list—what was I going to eat? Coffee elicited exhaustion; I knew that caffeine made me hyper, but the bean itself made me tired. Corn gave me a headache, stomachache, and a spacey feeling.

I was then tested for common inhalants—the things that we breathe in the environment. This, too, was very revealing. Chlorine caused fatigue and pulsating temples—even the tap water had to go! Formaldehyde, which is impregnated into synthetic fibers, brought on a headache and that foggy feeling again, as well as exhaustion and an increased pulse rate. This was an important link for me because I always felt tired and developed a mild headache when I was researching clothing stores for my weekly fashion column.

At this point, my very lifestyle and career were being challenged. It was hard to accept all of this information at once. But then they brought out one more test—for a yeast extract called *Candida albicans*. This experiment took 30 minutes.

Within ten minutes of this test, I had a dry cough and felt that old familiar sensation of panic and anxiety across my chest. A few minutes later, this turned into depression. Then my neck and shoulders became stiff, and the numbness and tingling in my arms and hands became severe. At last, all that I needed to know was revealed to me in black and white. I almost cried with relief that here, finally, was an answer. These reactions indicated that my "wholesome" diet and *candida* yeast were at the root of my physical symptoms.

Within three weeks of taking a specific substance to stamp out the *candida* yeast, and making the necessary dietary changes,

I began to feel better. The pain in my neck and shoulders, and the tingling down my arms, had diminished. I adhered very closely to my new dietary restrictions for several months—which was no mean feat, and added considerable stress to my busy lifestyle as a mother and newspaper columnist.

But my energy returned. I was no longer tired and worn out, and the great bonus was that I could eat as much as I wanted as long as I stayed away from *offending foods*. And, I *lost* weight. Most days I felt like a 21-year-old. My skin cleared up, and my brain and memory returned to normal clarity. My temperament and attitude toward life was one of joyous anticipation. This is how we're all supposed to feel!

All my symptoms had disappeared, never to return. I was charged with vitality and made the inner commitment that I was ready for a new direction. I didn't have to wait long.

After several months of being his patient, the allergist approached me and asked me to join his clinic. He realized that I had good communication skills, was compliant on the new program, had a medical background, and was keenly interested in the whole field of environmental medicine—so he asked me to become trained as his assistant and allergy-testing technician. I was delighted.

This involved an intense, year-long, total immersion program with much studying, training, and attendance at seminars. I was in total joy—I had found my life's purpose.

One morning I arrived at the clinic early. As I was working quietly at my desk, I noticed a bright light begin to form on the back wall of the testing room. As it began to get brighter, I felt intense heat in my own body. Suddenly, in the center of this expanded, blinding white light, the rarefied outline of a figure appeared—a presence, a radiant being, a messenger . . . an angel.

I stared, awestruck, as this presence spoke to me, not with words that I could hear out loud, but words that I could hear *within* me. "Behold the Angel. Will you do my work?" was what I heard. The effect of this presence seemed to pierce right through me to the core of my being. I sat and gazed in wonder. I wasn't afraid. It was as if I had met this presence before, and it had traveled with me throughout my life. Without words, I acknowledged that I would do "the work"—whatever it was—and in an instant, the vision disappeared.

I couldn't believe what had happened. Time stood still—what seemed like an eternity was actually a wink of an eye. I wanted to pinch myself to know that what I'd seen was real. I was in a state of euphoria and floated around the office like a puppet on a string. As I wandered around, completely elated, I was filled with the presence of love and inner knowing. That particular day gave me the opportunity to experience the deeper meaning of life on all levels, and to understand why we're put on this Earth.

As soon as the patients arrived at the clinic that day, I could see the auras, or electromagnetic fields, around them. And I seemed to know on a deeper level why they were coming to the clinic, what they had to tell me, and what I had to share with them. This was a powerful, compelling experience for which I wasn't fully prepared, and it heralded an infusion of the gifts of the spirit, which were to be bestowed upon me.

From then on, all I had to do was see a patient's name on the chart and I would immediately receive a flood of information about their treatment—which compounds to use, exactly where to start each treatment remedy, or anything else that was important to know. Fortunately, I had developed a comfortable rapport with the doctor, and as soon as I was able, I discussed the information I was being given with him. I will be forever grateful that he was open-minded and allowed me to communicate any of the impressions I experienced regarding his patients, and he was willing to incorporate this knowledge into his practice.

It took some time to ponder the significance of that experience in my office. What was the meaning of "Will you do my work?" My first thought was that there must be some very special work for me to do; or, could it be that the work I needed to do was on *myself?*

I immediately set out to become a more loving presence in my own life. This was a transformational concept, as I instantly became conscious and present in every single interaction, every moment of the day. I knew that each person in the clinic would be the test of this commitment. They could be frustrated, irritable, weary, and lacking in hope, and I had to see beyond their outer behavior and recognize that they were precious souls traveling on the same path that I was. My role was to be present and loving, and to visualize them healthy and well.

From that pivotal morning on, things became very accelerated in the clinic. We were able to bypass some of the slow, laborious treatments and simplify our approaches, because the doctor himself was becoming more intuitive. We used to get together for a couple of hours on the weekends to intuit protocols and new techniques. What a team we were!

It was extremely fulfilling work, and these were high times. But I was also getting exhausted. The clinic opened early, and we would see countless people every day, month after month, with no relief in sight. I was getting intuitive nudges that soon it would be time to leave the clinic, which made me sad, but I also realized that it had to be done.

The next step was revealed to me in a powerful dream shortly after I left the clinic. For the previous three years, along with everything else that I was doing, I'd been studying relaxation therapy. God knows I needed to relax! I discovered that I had a talent for creating individual, guided-imagery audiotapes, which helped adults and children to relax, sleep better, and feel more positive about life. So, one morning, I awoke from a very graphic dream that showed me a complete set of audiotapes designed to help children feel positive and loved—which is the basis of good health! I was also shown in the dream that these audiotapes would be teamed with a cuddly doll in the shape of an angel. At last, it was time to further understand the meaning of "Will you do my work?"

I opened a small office, and many people asked to have individualized audiotapes created for their own needs. Many of my clients were children who had a variety of ailments and concerns such as head injuries, burns, amputations, divorce, abuse, sleeplessness, and the aftereffects of cancer treatments. It was always a pleasure to create audiotapes for these kids, and I felt that the words on the tapes were spiritually inspired. I called them *Sleep Talking*® tapes.

After a few years at my office, I met a naturopathic physician who was aware of my intuitive abilities. He invited me to join his practice as an allergy-testing technician and welcomed my input. While I was at this clinic, I had the chance to witness some of the eclectic treatment modalities offered by naturopathic physicians, and to see the benefits of injectable and intravenous vitamins. We would often see patients with severe chronic illnesses—chronic fatigue syndrome (CFS), cancer, or other serious conditions—who benefited tremendously from these injections.

Eventually I felt compelled to forge my own path, focusing on my medical-intuitive ability. At first, I resisted it, feeling that it was only appropriate to be used in a professional medical setting. But I could never resist the desire to help when it was needed: I jotted down programs for people on napkins in restaurants, or made a suggestion in passing when it was required. It just evolved—and people all over the world started to contact me.

To me, medical intuition is a very simple, natural, and straightforward ability that anyone can learn. I tend to always see the body in a state of wellness. I don't dwell on what's negative or out of balance; rather, I focus on what might be helpful to correct the situation.

Basically, I consider my work to be an introduction to the healing journey.

(From *The Body "Knows,"* Hay House, 2001)

Alberto Villoldo, Ph.D.

© Christine Paul

Alberto Villoldo, Ph.D., the author of *Shaman, Healer, Sage; Mending the Past and Healing the Future with Soul Retrieval;* and *The Four Insights,* is a psychologist and medical anthropologist who comes from a long line of Earthkeepers from the Amazon and the Andes. He has studied the healing practices of the Amazon and Andean shamans for more than 25 years.

Villoldo directs The Four Winds Society, where he instructs individuals throughout the world in the practice of energy medicine and soul retrieval. He has training centers in New England; California; the U.K.; the Netherlands; and Park City, Utah.

An avid skier, hiker, and mountaineer, he leads annual expeditions to the Amazon and the Andes to work with the wisdom teachers of the Americas.

Website: **www.thefourwinds.com**

THE JOY OF LIVING

Soul is the best word we have for that essential part of ourselves that seems to have preceded our entry into this world, yet also endures beyond our lifetime. In order to heal the soul, I must go fishing in the deepest waters of my psyche, where I haven't gone before. In soul retrieval, I neither dissect nor deny my lost soul parts—instead I acknowledge and heal them, and integrate them back into the whole of my being.

~

Here's a story from my own life, which will give you a sense of the dimensions that soul retrieval addresses:

I was born in Cuba, and when I was ten years old, there was a revolution in the country. War broke out, and no one knew whom the enemy was, since everyone spoke the same language and dressed alike. One day my father gave me his .45 caliber U.S. Army Colt pistol. He showed me how to use it, sitting me down by the front door of our home and explaining, "When I'm gone, you're the man of the house, and you have to protect your mother, sister, and grandmother. If anybody tries to break in, shoot through the door!"

I sat by the door for several weeks listening to gunfire going off blocks away, until three militiamen finally came to the house. At first they knocked on the door, and when no one answered they tried to kick it in. I asked myself, *Do I shoot through the door, or do I wait for them to come inside?* Then I did what any ten-year-old would do: I put the gun down and went to the window. One of the men made eye contact with me through the glass, saw a frightened little boy, and told the others, "Come, there's no one here. Let's go."

That day I lost my childhood. I grew up very quickly during those few weeks sitting with death by the door. I forgot how to just be a kid, and instead became a serious little man. And I also became terrified of strangers—had recurring nightmares of people breaking down the door to our home and taking all my loved ones.

By journeying—a unique state of consciousness that is entered through guided meditations and breathing exercises—I was able to go back and revisit the boy who faced death when he was ten. I retrieved little Alberto and told him that everything would be okay, that I'd look after him, and that he was never going to have to be burdened with the survival of his family.

When I recovered my 10-year-old self in my early 30s, I got my childhood back. I was able to give up my constant seriousness and mistrust of others, and to stop seeing everything as a life-or-death crisis. I stopped being in survival mode and began to experience the joy of living.

(From *Mending the Past and Healing the Future with Soul Retrieval,* Hay House, 2005)

Doreen Virtue, Ph.D.

www.photographybycheryl.com

Doreen Virtue, Ph.D., is a fourth-generation metaphysician and clairvoyant doctor of psychology who works with the angelic, elemental, and ascended-master realms. Doreen is the author of numerous best-selling books and products, including the international best-sellers *The Lightworker's Way, Healing with the Angels, Archangels & Ascended Masters,* and *Daily Guidance from Your Angels.* She's been featured on *Oprah,* CNN, *Good Morning America,* and in newspapers and magazines worldwide.

Doreen teaches classes related to her books and frequently gives audience angel readings. Website: **www.angeltherapy.com**.

Reconnecting
with My
Twin Flame

I was amazed that I hadn't noticed the fairies until I reached my adult years. Looking back at my childhood, I remember clearly seeing deceased people and the evidence of guardian angels. I remembered when my family moved (when I was two years old) to our home on Craner Avenue in North Hollywood (in L.A.'s San Fernando Valley). It was there that I had my first "mediumistic" experiences—although I didn't know it at the time.

All I knew was that I *saw* people, opaque and very alive looking—whom others didn't see. One evening, for instance, I called my mother into my bedroom and told her that "the people" kept staring at me. I could see adults, but I didn't recognize them as deceased relatives. They were complete strangers, and I could see them as clearly as I could see my mother. She didn't see anything, though, and told me that since she and my father had been in the living room watching television, the people I was seeing must have been images from the TV set reflected in my bedroom window. But that didn't make any sense at all. People on television moved and spoke. These people just stood there and stared.

I had some very deep friendships with the other children on Craner Avenue: David, Jody, Colleen, and I played together daily. I also spent a lot of time with my best friend, Stephanie, whose parents managed the apartment building at the end of our cul-de-sac. Her upstairs neighbor, Steven, was one of the cutest boys I'd ever seen. From age five onward, I had a hopeless crush on him, but he never seemed to notice me, since I was ten years younger. So, I was relegated to staring at Steven from afar, telling Stephanie how I wished that he would notice me.

Steven and I only interacted a few times. One time he held an impromptu neighborhood show in which he demonstrated his ventriloquism talents with his Jerry Mahoney doll. I sat transfixed in the audience of kids in a neighbor's garage, watching Steven talk to the doll. Afterward, I asked him endless questions about the mechanisms of throwing your voice, and how the doll's mouth and eyes moved. I admired him so much—my first crush!

Many years later, well into adulthood and single once again, I had one of my "conversations" with the heavenly fairies. I voiced: *I am truly happy, and so grateful for all that I have. When I find my soul mate, I will have the life of my dreams.*

"We will help you with that endeavor, Doreen," the fairies responded. "You will soon meet your soul mate. We promise."

I can feel the truth of that, yes. I know that he will soon be in my life, I concurred, but also couldn't help reliving a lifetime of unexpressed pain. I thought back to Steven, the cute boy next door on Craner Avenue whom I'd had such a huge crush on but who had never paid me any notice. I had a freeze-frame photograph of him in my mind that symbolized my unrequited love: It was the memory of him standing on a grassy mound next to his apartment building's swimming pool. He wore cutoff shorts and was barefoot. He had no idea, I suppose, that I was watching him at that moment, because he stared off into the distance. Steven seemed to be in his own world.

Not too long after this, I walked into the reception area of a yoga studio in Laguna Beach in order to take a class, and several of my friends greeted me. As I was talking with Sue, a psychotherapist friend of mine, I heard a male voice behind her say, "Hi, Doreen!" I looked up and glanced at the man addressing me. "It's me, Steven Farmer. Remember me?"

Of course I remembered him. I'd first met him about a year before and had expressed interest, but hadn't seemed to get any back in return. For a year I'd thought about him, but each time I asked our mutual acquaintance Johnna about him, I'd felt rejected. It seemed as if Johnna was asking him out on my behalf, and that he was turning her (me) down, so I just smiled at him and went back to my conversation with Sue. During the class, I didn't give Steven a second glance, since I'd written him off months earlier as being "chronically disinterested in me."

The yoga class was wonderful, and I left feeling euphoric. Two days later, I stopped into the yoga studio to drop off some decks of my *Healing with the Angels Oracle Cards*, which Johnna sold at her shop. Steven's daughter, Nicole, was working behind the desk, and she gave me a big smile and hug. Nicole and I had gotten to know each other over the past year, and I genuinely liked her.

She and I seemed to have similar outlooks on a lot of life issues, including dating and men. As I was getting ready to leave, Nicole remarked, "My dad said something about you after the yoga class last week."

I stopped and turned to face her. Nicole was incredibly lovely, with delicate porcelain skin, baby blue eyes, and naturally blonde hair. She looked just like a beautiful, opalescent, incarnated fairy. I could even see her translucent dragonfly wings beating behind her shoulder blades.

Nicole continued, "My dad said, 'I never realized that Doreen was so attractive.'"

I looked at Nicole and felt a strong wave of happiness. I wrote my home and cell-phone numbers on a paper, and handed it to her. "Then please tell your dad to call me and ask me out," I said with a smile.

"I will," she said.

I didn't put much energy into thinking about Steven Farmer, due to not hearing from him or seeing him throughout the year. Besides, I was busy creating a new deck of oracle cards called *Healing with the Fairies*. The fairies were busily instructing me about which words to write in the guidebook accompanying the cards.

So when I received a message on my machine from Steven a few days later, I was actually surprised—pleasantly so. His message asked me to join him for breakfast, brunch, or a mid-morning coffee and a beach walk on Sunday. My choice. However, I knew that I'd probably be too nervous to eat, and I also don't drink coffee, so I called him back and made a date to meet him for a bottle of water and a beach walk.

I woke up Sunday morning feeling as anxious as a schoolgirl going on her first date. My nervousness resulted in my being ten minutes late for our agreed-upon meeting at Diedrich's Coffee on Pacific Coast Highway. First, I had to figure out what to wear. Through prayer, I felt guided to select a denim skirt and beige tank top, with a swimsuit underneath in case we decided to go for a swim. Second, I had to contend with Sunday-morning traffic. And third, the only parking space I could find was three blocks from Diedrich's.

By the time I walked into the coffee shop, I was a nervous wreck. I breathed deeply to center myself, looking around for Steven. He was nowhere within the coffee shop, so I walked outside. I worried, "What if I don't remember what he looks like?" After all, I really hadn't looked at him closely in almost a year.

But my fears were unfounded. As I stepped outside onto Diedrich's patio, a man called out, "Doreen!" There sat a stunningly handsome silver-haired man waving to me. Could that be Steven? He sported a "Laguna Yoga" T-shirt, and stood up to hug me hello. I felt both comforted and flustered.

Steven asked if I wanted anything to drink or eat before going on our beach walk. I declined, since my throat felt tight with anticipation, and I didn't know if I could eat or drink. I'd learned that each astrological sign has an "Achilles heel" somewhere in their bodies, and as a Taurus, mine was the throat. This area revealed my unexpressed emotions, and while I almost never got sick, I'd lose my voice now and then. At that moment, standing next to the awesome Steven Farmer, I felt quiet and content.

We walked across the street to Main Beach and began walking south along the surf. Steven began telling me about himself: He held a master's degree in counseling psychology.

"Me, too!" I said. "Where did you get your degree?"

"At Chapman University."

"Me, too!" I said again.

Steven told me that he'd written several books about child abuse, including the best-selling work *Adult Children of Abusive Parents*. I explained that my clinical specialty had been eating disorders, particularly for those who had a history of child abuse. My doctoral dissertation had been on the link between child abuse and eating disorders, which had turned into my first Hay House book, *Losing Your Pounds of Pain*. We also discovered that we both had two of the same publishers, CompCare and Lowell House.

He asked what books I was currently writing. I told him that I was in the midst of two books—one a New Age work, and the other a more mainstream book, *The Care and Feeding of Indigo Children*.

Would it scare Steven if I told him that I was writing a book called *Healing with the Fairies?* I decided to tell him the truth. After all, I was looking for a man who accepted my spiritual pursuits.

"You believe in fairies?" he asked.

Oops, I thought, *he's judging me.*

Steven continued, "I just attended a workshop about Celtic devas and fairies on Friday. I think that it's so neat that you're writing about them."

Wow!

Then Steven told me about his studies in shamanism. His beliefs in life after death mirrored and complemented my own so much that I felt like I was floating. "What's your sun sign?" he asked me.

"I'm a Taurus."

"Oh, my darlin'!" he exclaimed, putting his strong arm around my shoulders. "I've always been told that I should be with a Taurus lady."

"What sign are you?"

"I'm a Capricorn." Now I was in shock. All the astrologers and astrology books had recommended that I should be with a Capricorn man. Their advice had always frustrated me because I'd never felt a chemical attraction toward any Capricorns. But I was completely attracted to Steven, and the more he talked, the more

I felt myself melting in response to his words.

"I thought Johnna told me you were a Cancer sign," I remarked, as we sat on a granite rock near the Surf and Sand Hotel.

"Nope, I'm a Capricorn, with Taurus rising," he stated.

"Amazing," I replied. "I'm a Taurus, with Capricorn rising." We walked in comfortable silence for a few paces, and then continued sharing personal information with each other. Steven told me how his two daughters, Nicole, 20, and Catherine, 18, had lived with him for the past several years. His relationship with them reminded me of my own experiences with my sons, Chuck, 22, and Grant, 20. I had been friends with Steven's daughter, Nicole, for the past year, and my sons had gotten to know and like her, too. Steven and I seemed to have so much in common!

But I was still bothered by the nagging question of why Steven had taken a year to ask me out on a date. However, it became clear when he told me about the turmoil in his life over the past 12 months: His two brothers had passed away within one month of each other, right after we had met in yoga class. Then, a few months later, he closed a retail business that he'd run for several years. "I didn't feel emotionally ready for a relationship until just recently," he explained.

We walked back toward the beach in front of Heisler Park and found an inviting spot to rest. The sun was warm and glowing, and the waves looked so appealing. "Want to go for a swim?" I asked Steven.

He said, "Sure."

We jumped and played in the surf like two kids, side by side. I felt too shy to touch Steven, and he kept his distance from me, too. But inside, my heart was opening to him in a new and wondrous way.

Steven and I returned to our spot on the sand to dry off in the warm afternoon sun. He opened his waist pack and pulled out some papers. "I want to read you some things," he said. Steven then began reading me beautiful poetry! His voice was strong and expressive, and he'd stop occasionally to look me in the eyes before continuing his recitation.

When we parted later in the day, we hugged warmly. The next day, I went to Los Angeles to meet with television producers who were interested in creating a show with me as the host. My sons went with me, and we had fun discussing program ideas with the producers. We returned to Orange County feeling positive about the meeting.

I walked into my condominium and checked my answering machine. "I don't know if you've had a chance to read your e-mail yet," said a deep male voice, "but I was wondering if you'd go to the movies with me tonight." It was Steven, asking me out! What a perfect way to end a glorious day.

It was a warm and lovely evening, and we drove with the convertible top down to a movie theater in Aliso Viejo. We were on our way to see *Almost Famous,* a movie about rock-and-roll that I'd wanted to see.

I realized that, although I knew about Steven's present work as a spiritual psychotherapist and author, I didn't know much about his upbringing.

"So where were you born and raised?" I asked.

"I was born in Cedar Rapids, Iowa, in 1948."

Steven was ten years older than I was. *Perfect,* I thought. I tended to be attracted to men in that age range.

He continued, "Then, in 1960, our family moved to North Hollywood, California."

"You're kidding!" I said. "In 1960, *my* family moved to North Hollywood."

"Amazing!" he said. "Whereabouts did you live?"

I replied, "Near Victory and Vineland."

"Hmm, that's just about the area where I lived."

I continued, "I lived on a little cul-de-sac called Craner Avenue."

Steven looked at me and exclaimed in amazement, "Wait a minute! *Our* family lived on Craner Avenue!"

My mind reeled and my heart leapt as I realized who he was. "You're the guy! You're the guy!" I was practically yelling.

"What?"

"You're the guy who lived at the end of the block in the apartments on Craner Avenue! You're Steven, the guy I had my first crush on! I used to stare at you, but you never seemed to notice me—I guess because I was so much younger than you." Since I hadn't seen Steven in more than 30 years, I'd had no idea up until now that he was the boy next door from my childhood days.

Luckily, we'd just pulled into the movie theater's parking lot, because I doubt that Steven or I could have coherently driven the car any longer. We were both in shock.

"Are you sure?" he asked.

I then described details about Craner Avenue that distinguished it from other streets. We compared notes on our neighbors, who included the talent agent of Jay North (aka Dennis the Menace) and a man who collected drag-racing cars. We were clearly talking about the same street and the same time frame.

I was reunited with my very first crush! How romantic that I'd experienced love at first sight with the same guy—twice in one lifetime! The movie was a blur to both of us. We didn't even touch our popcorn, but instead, held each other close throughout the entire two hours.

After the movie, we drove back to Laguna Beach, still wondering what all of this meant. Steven and I obviously had much in common, and were deeply attracted to one another on many levels. And now this mystical twist in which we discovered that he was the boy next door! I felt the hand of the angels, fairies, and our deceased loved ones playing a part in our reunion.

A few days later, I was getting ready for my third date with Steven. He arrived right on time—a good sign, I thought.

We hugged warmly, and then he said, "I think we both know where this is going, and I just want to get everything out in the open. I brought a list of all my bad characteristics so you can know what you're getting into." I laughed with joy at Steven's openness and expressiveness. How refreshing he was!

Steven's list of "bad" traits seemed mild and normal, almost complementary to my own negative traits. "We all have shadows,"

Steven said. "It's just important to be aware of them and not let them rule you." I couldn't have agreed more.

When he was done reading his list, I said, "That's all? Where are the bad parts?" He chuckled and gave me a big hug.

Then I shared my own list of shadows with him. Steven didn't run away. In fact, he sat closer to me when I was done. He looked at me with sparkling eyes, and I thought, *Oh, we're falling in love!* I didn't fight the thought or the emotion, feeling very safe with Steven, like I'd known him a million years.

We shared a beautiful evening together. The next day, I went to the beach and sat on a quartz rock to meditate and talk with the fairies. *I know that you were behind my reconnection with Steven,* I said to them, *and I just want to thank you.*

Intuitively, the fairies let me know that they *had* helped orchestrate many of the synchronicities surrounding our meeting. However, we also had help from many others in heaven, including Steven's deceased mother and brother, my Grandma Pearl, Archangel Michael, and our guardian angels. "Thank you all!" I exclaimed, with gratitude and joy filling my heart. The fairies confirmed that Steven and I had shared many lifetimes together.

Within two weeks, Steven and I were inseparable. We continued to learn about our commonalities, and the message was clear: We were more than soul mates. We were "twin flames," a term given to people who are from the same soul, and who separate into distinctly male and female personas. Sometimes twin flames didn't incarnate together; it was common for one to be in a body, and the other to act as a spirit guide.

We learned from the "I Am" teachings of the ascended masters that when twin flames incarnate together, it often signals their last incarnation on Earth. It's an opportunity for both partners to form an earthly union to create one final "hurrah" while in their last life here.

Steven and I had both spent our lifetimes working toward purposeful, meaningful aims. We were both passionate lightworkers, committed to helping usher in a new age of peace. We were both givers and helpers, personally and professionally. In our prior relationships, we'd experienced imbalances of being the "giver" who was matched with a "taker." These sorts of relationships can be draining for the giver, and they can make the taker feel guilty. "Two givers in a relationship is ideal," Steven said to me, "and that's what you and I have."

We discovered that there had been many instances in our lives when Steven and I could have met. Starting from childhood, we could have become friends and begun a lifetime relationship. Then, in 1988, when we were both with CompCare Publishers, we could have met. Or, when we both lived on the Newport Beach, California, peninsula in 1993 and were both single, we could have had a relationship blossom. Or, we could have met as students of Chapman University. The list of our life intersections went on and on.

Apparently, soul mates are brought together continually, until the couple finally connects. At first, Steven and I grieved over our lifetime apart. "We could have avoided so much pain in our other relationships if only we'd gotten together earlier in our lives!" we told each other. But ultimately, we decided that the timing just hadn't been right up till now. We both needed to grow and learn from other relationships.

⌒

Steven and I grew increasingly close and fell even more deeply in love. I was enthralled at being in a love relationship where I could openly discuss my conversations with the angels and fairies. We frequently spoke to Archangel Michael together, and we also participated in spiritual ceremonies and meditations.

We'd frequently say to each other, "I never knew that love could be so wonderful!" Steven began accompanying me to workshops, and frequently co-led seminars. I was no longer lonely while traveling, and I renewed my commitment to giving workshops worldwide.

We consecrated our union in a spiritual ceremony presided over by a shamanic teacher named Jade Wah'oo. It was a beautiful ritual in which Steven and I professed our commitment to spending our life together and told one another about the depth of our love.

⌒

One day not too long after our ceremony, I remarked to Steven, "You know what would be really fun to do since it's Saturday and there isn't much traffic today? How about driving to our childhood neighborhood in North Hollywood?"

Steven grinned and readily agreed. "It's only a half hour from the airport," he said.

I hadn't been to the neighborhood since I was 10 years old, and Steven hadn't been there since he was 16. As we turned right onto Craner Avenue, I felt like I'd traveled into a time tunnel. Nothing had changed!

As we pulled in front of my childhood home, I felt like I was in a daze, realizing that even the landscaping hadn't been altered in the last 30 years. Steven and I climbed out of his truck, walking arm in arm.

The situation started to feel even more surreal when I realized that both of us felt equal amounts of shock upon seeing our old neighborhood. I'd been with other people who had been through similar experiences, but I was always able to remain detached and supportive because I wasn't directly involved. But on this occasion, both Steven and I were on the same wavelength—dealing with a real déjà-vu scenario.

I stared at my childhood home, the place where I'd first consciously had clairvoyant experiences. I looked at the hedge on our neighbor's lawn where I'd once seen a man crouching—but when I'd told my friends about the man, they couldn't see him. The hedge reminded me of the pain I'd suffered because my clairvoyance had made me feel different from other people.

Steven listened empathetically as I brought up my childhood memories. On the one hand, I was raised in a loving and empowering family system—imagine having parents who encouraged the use of affirmations, visualization, and prayer to heal and manifest! Yet, in spite of all these advantages, I suffered because of my sensitivity to other children's tauntings ("You're weird!"), and my parents' lack of acknowledgment of my clairvoyance.

Steven embraced me tightly and said, "Everything's okay now. I'm here, and I love you so deeply." He looked me in the eyes, ensuring that I truly heard his words, and I felt the depth of his profound love.

We walked to his apartment building, and I watched Steven's breath deepen and his eyes drift far away. He was remembering, reliving, a time long ago. Since I had spent my childhood playing at his apartment complex with my girlfriend Stephanie, I joined in the remembrance.

There was the mosaic pathway that I remembered playing on! It sure had shrunk in size since I was a child. And there was the grassy mound where my mind held the frozen memory of Steven standing so many years earlier.

"Sweetheart," I asked, "can you stand right here?" Since Steven knew about my memory, he readily agreed. He stood in the exact same position that I recalled, looking away from me toward the pool. My breath quickened at the sight—so familiar, but with both of us taller and older. Then I approached him from behind until I walked around to face him. Steven pulled me close and warmly kissed me.

I felt my breathing change radically so that it extended deep into my belly. I hadn't realized how shallow my breath was until that moment. Steven's affection opened my heart, like Prince Charming's kiss awakening Sleeping Beauty. I felt a glacier melt that had surrounded my heart since it had felt rebuffed by Steven—my very first love—so many years ago. My early experience of unrequited love had set the tone for my entire love life, and I knew the pattern was now healed.

Steven was my first . . . and is my last . . . love.

(From *Healing with the Fairies,* Hay House, 2001)

Wyatt Webb

Wyatt Webb, the author of *It's Not about the Horse* (with Cindy Pearlman) and *What to Do When You Don't Know What to Do,* survived 15 years in the music industry as an entertainer, touring the country 30 weeks a year. Realizing he was practically killing himself due to drug and alcohol addictions, Wyatt sought help, which led him to quit the entertainment industry. He began what is now a 25-year career as a therapist.

Eventually, Wyatt became one of the most creative, unconventional, and sought-after therapists in the country. Today he's the founder and leader of the Equine Experience at Miraval Life in Balance™, one of the world's premier resorts, which is located in Tucson, Arizona.

A SENSE OF
CONNECTION

One of the deepest connections I've felt within the past five to ten years of my life occurred in April 2002 when I had the opportunity to spend three days in New York City, presenting a workshop for the staff of a national magazine. The day I arrived, a friend of mine, a documentary filmmaker named Barry Boyle, greeted me at my hotel in Times Square and we proceeded to go to Ground Zero, the former site of the World Trade Center towers.

The trip from Times Square to the neighborhood where the towers had been was an event in and of itself. It was my first trip on a subway, and I'd heard all kinds of terrible stories over the years about the subway system. None of them turned out to be true for me. Beneath the streets of New York City, I consistently connected with people.

I was wearing a big hat, and one lady tapped me on the shoulder and said, "You might want to hold on to the support bar. I'd hate to see you get that beautiful hat knocked off." I asked her what tipped her off that I wasn't a veteran of subway travel, and this gave six or eight people an opportunity to laugh with each other. Conversations continued to occur with people I'd never met in my life, and people smiled at me as I made my way toward Ground Zero. This had been my experience in New York on two previous occasions, so maybe we get what we ask for. I was certainly in a place of being open to the people in New York City, and they responded in a most favorable way.

What occurred at the end of that subway ride was one of the most meaningful experiences of my life, and I'll never forget it as long as I live. We came up out of the subway and took a cab to the cordoned-off viewing area that surrounded Ground Zero. The first thing I noticed was how clean the place was. It was nothing like the horrendous debris I'd seen on TV. Other than the absence of those huge towers and some construction around the area, there was no evidence that this catastrophic event had occurred. I thought to myself, *How capable and incredible of people to come in and restore some semblance of order to an area that had been so completely devastated.*

The church that sits to the right of Ground Zero was spotless, and the fence around it was covered with literally hundreds of thousands of expressions of sympathy, love, and respect for those who'd lost their lives. I remember thinking that approximately 3,000 people had lost their lives that day, which in turn somehow provided hundreds of thousands of people an opportunity to connect as fellow participants on this journey on this planet.

As we walked toward the ramp that led to Ground Zero, I realized that even if I spent a week there, it would have been impossible for me to count all the cards, bouquets, ribbons, and plaques of acknowledgment. God only knows how many heartfelt notes had been written and sent. I remember feeling incredible sadness as I reached up and touched the signatures on the plywood walls that lined the ramp. I remember walking out to the edge of the barricade and the ramp and looking over into the empty space that had housed those two magnificent buildings, which in turn housed all those wonderful souls who were simply living their lives on a daily basis. I remember Barry looking at me and saying, "I've never seen a sadder look on anybody's face than when you looked over the edge into where the towers were."

I remember thinking to myself in the midst of my sadness that I definitely felt a sense of connection, due to the multitude of expressions from people all over the world who, in their journey to that place, had done what they could to say, "I'm sorry this happened." I wish we could get the message that this opportunity to express something from our hearts exists on a daily basis, and that we need not wait for a tragedy as an excuse to express our feelings toward our fellow human beings.

All of those souls had given those of us who were left behind an opportunity to express something from our hearts. Does that make up for their loss? Of course not. But there seemed to be some spiritual justice involved with what had happened, and was happening as I was there, and what must happen there on a daily basis for people from all over the world. It seemed as if every country on the planet had been represented there by expressions of sympathy and support.

As Barry and I stood quietly looking at the emptiness of the space, a young man and his wife came up to us. He was about 6'8", but she was in a wheelchair and couldn't see over the four-and-a-half-foot barrier that kept people from entering the site. What occurred next brought tears to my eyes. This gentle giant bent all the way down to the ground, balancing himself on one leg and easing himself back between her legs. He placed her legs around his waist, she wrapped her arms around his neck; and this big, strong man stood up with her and walked to the edge of the barricades with her on his back so that she might see Ground Zero for herself.

When I talk about the opportunity to connect and the sweetness of that, I remember that day in April 2002, and I will continue to remember it for the rest of my life.

(From *What to Do When You Don't Know What to Do,* Hay House, 2006)

Hank Wesselman, Ph.D.

Steven Stafford

Anthropologist **Hank Wesselman, Ph.D.**, received his doctoral degree from the University of California at Berkeley and has worked with an international group of scientists for much of the past 35 years, exploring Eastern Africa's Great Rift Valley in search of answers to the mystery of human origins. He currently resides in Northern California, where he teaches at American River College and Sierra College and offers experiential workshops and presentations in core shamanism worldwide. He's the author of *Spiritwalker, Medicinemaker, Visionseeker, The Journey to the Sacred Garden,* and *Spirit Medicine* (with his wife Jill Kuykendall, RPT).

THE CARETAKER
OF MY GARDEN

My spiritual awakening began on the island of Hawai'i through a series of spontaneous visionary encounters with Nainoa, a fellow mystic and kahuna initiate who lives 5,000 years in the future. . . .

～

Several years had passed since I had participated in any formal training in shamanic practice, and in the interim, I had become aware that anthropologist Michael Harner had created an advanced program in which an ongoing, established group of individuals would meet for a week twice each year for three years. I had run into Harner at some anthropology meetings the previous March, and he had told me that a new group was being formed, encouraging me to call up his Foundation for Shamanic Studies to enroll. I followed his advice and was accepted into the new group.

It was during this first training session that I was able to further explore my personal place of power, my secret garden in the dream world, and once again, I received some real surprises.

In my shamanic journeywork, I experience the spirit worlds as a great three-leveled system with worlds above this one and worlds below. These realities are dreamlike and subjective in nature, and are simultaneously levels of awareness and levels of experience By shifting my awareness, I effectively change my level of experience, in the process shifting from one level of reality to another. This reveals that these realities can also be understood as levels of consciousness, including, of course, the level of ordinary reality in which we live our lives on an ongoing, day-to-day basis.

In the classic Upper Worlds are found the luminous levels inhabited by the gods and goddesses, the spiritual heroes and heroines of the past, and those higher powers beyond solar and planetary development. Paradise. Below the physical plane of everyday existence are the mythic Lower Worlds—the great cosmic regions visited by shamans for tens of millennia in order to access the spirits of nature and to connect with mystical power, among other things. In between the Lower and Upper Worlds are the Middle Worlds of human dreaming. These are the places we go into when we dream at night, and many cultures believe that these are also the levels in which we find ourselves immediately after the death experience. It is in these levels that my secret garden is located.

As Nainoa had revealed, the ordinary-reality aspect of this place is on the island of Hawai'i, a site at Kealakekua Bay where I used to go with my family on a daily basis when we lived in the islands. An opportunity to visit its dream aspect appeared later in the week. Once again, I was lying on my Navajo rug, with Michael and Christina, one of the seminar teachers, providing the powerful assist with the drum. I merged with the sound, instructed my *ku* (the body-mind) to open the inner doorway, and as the power sensations swept into me, the primary focus of my conscious awareness shifted from here to there. It was very fast, like changing channels on a television.

My vision came up as I arrived on the massive stone platform of the *heiau*—a prehistoric Hawaiian temple that overlies a dense concentration of *mana* (power) in the earth below it. I looked around me and took in the full experience of this marvelous place. All of my senses were kicking in so that my experience of this place was becoming increasingly vivid. I could smell the salt of the ocean and the celery-like scent of the trees from the forest behind the *heiau*. I could hear the light sea breeze rattling the palms, as well as the ceaseless pulse of the waves breaking on the beach. I could feel the sun on my skin and the roughness of the lava stones under my feet.

An idea appeared within my mind. It would be nice to have a house in my garden. I had always wanted to have a place at the beach, and this seemed like a perfect opportunity. I went over to the slab of smooth black basalt that served me as an altar and lay down on it. I closed my eyes and erased my thoughts. Then I created a visualization—an image of the house just as I would like it to be. I began with a stone house platform much like the *heiau* but smaller. I imagined a crew of workers constructing it under the direction of a master stoneworker at the edge of the pond near a big tamarind I knew was growing there. Then I proceeded to design the house on the platform, and as the thought-form was transformed into reality by the same construction crew, I drew on the *mana* of the *heiau* to invest the image with power.

For long moments, I dreamed my house into existence, crowning the edifice with a tall thatched roof in the Hawaiian style. Then another thought appeared. I would need a caretaker to live in my house when I was not there. At this instant, I recalled Hakai, the chief gardener, saying that there was a powerful spirit that lived in his garden. I cleared my mind and put out a request to the spirit in my garden—that it provide a caretaker for my house. Then I opened my eyes, rose from the altar, and walked over to the edge of the *heiau*.

There, beyond the pond, was another smaller stone platform surmounted by my house, partially concealed by the trees. I could clearly see part of its tall, thatched roof as well as a section of a broad lanai. Excitement rose within me. The magic seemed to have worked. This would be my personal getaway place in the Middle World of dream where I could go to restore myself. I recalled Hakai saying that the garden could also be a useful place in which to do healing work for others.

I descended the stone steps of the *heiau* and walked around the pond, noting that there were a few orange flowers from the *kou* trees floating on its surface. I paused and plucked a scarlet hibiscus blossom from a bush and placed it on the water, an offering to the water spirit. Then I strode into the shade of the trees and approached my house for the first time.

I climbed the stone steps and unlatched the gate, surveying the house with satisfaction. It was just as I had imagined it. I crossed the lanai and opened the door. My eyes roved with delight over the details of the central room, from the smooth hardwood floor to the exposed, carved wooden beams holding up the roof. Along one side was a raised sleeping platform covered with finely woven pandanus mats, and in the floor's center was a rectangular, recessed fire pit for cooking, and heating oneself on cool nights. I walked over to look out one of the windows, and there, on a smaller stone platform near the house, I saw the dream aspect of the spirit stone, its pointed end crowned with several white shell *leis*. On a low altar before it was a scarlet hibiscus blossom. Surprise surged through me. I hadn't put it there . . . then who . . .?

At this moment, I became aware of a presence, and turning, I saw a woman standing backlit in the doorway behind me. She was holding a large, flat wooden bowl or tray filled with what appeared to be fresh lychees. I had never met another human being in my spirit garden before, and my first take was to wonder if someone else had found their way into this place in their dreaming.

I made a gesture of welcome, and she moved gracefully into the room. Now I could see her clearly. Before me stood a woman of medium height with a *lei* of ferns and orange flowers from the *kou* trees wrapped around her head. Her dark hair was worn long, concealing most of her shoulders and chest. A colorful *pareu* was wrapped around her lower body in the Tahitian style. Her dark eyes were regardingly me solemnly. She was not a young girl, nor was she old. She was quite beautiful, with classic Polynesian features. There was something vaguely familiar about her. It was as though we had met before, but I couldn't recall when or where.

"Welcome," I said, somewhat formally. "My name is Hank Wesselman, and I think of this place as my secret garden, as my personal place of power in the dream world to which I come from time to time to accomplish various things. Might I inquire as to who you are and how you found your way here?" As I said these words, a memory from my childood suddenly emerged from my *ku*, a recollection of a visit to the Metropolitan Museum of Art in New York. This was (and is) one of my favorite places. As a boy, I was captivated by its antiquities, and especially the Egyptian collections.

The Caretaker of My Garden

I must have been about eight or nine years old when my mother and I found ourselves upstairs in the section of the museum that holds the paintings of the French Impressionists and Post-Impressionists. My mother was a painter, and she introduced me that afternoon to Renoir and Monet, Pissarro and van Gogh. But there was one painting in that great collection that drew me beyond all the others—Paul Gauguin's image of the two Tahitian women. One of them was standing, bare breasted, holding a large, flat platter of fruit or flowers.

All this passed through my mind in an instant as I realized that the woman standing before me strongly resembled the girl in Gauguin's painting. Then the moment passed as she stooped and placed her bowl on a low table, her motion parting her hair and revealing her breasts. Like the girl in the painting, her nipples were almost the same color as the fruit. Then she stood once more, her dark eyes regarding me with gravity.

"Bonjour, monsieur. Je m'appelle Tehura," she replied in French, reinforcing my growing conviction that this was indeed a Tahitian woman and that she could well be the woman from the painting. "My name is Tehura, and I have come at your request. How may I be of service to you?" I was stunned. I had momentarily forgotten my request to the spirit of my garden. *The caretaker of my property had arrived.* I accessed my limited knowledge of French and asked her if she spoke English. For the first time, she smiled, her face filling with light.

"But of course. Long ago, when I was young girl," she began in somewhat broken English, "I had a lover, an American sailor who came to my island. He taught me to speak the English." She paused and looked around the room approvingly. *"Quelle belle maison*—what a beautiful house."

I reached down and took one of the lychees from her tray. I cracked its thin, spikey shell, exposing the glistening, white fruit within. I popped it into my mouth, savoring its slightly astringent, grapefruitlike flavor before spitting out the shining black seed and tossing it out the window. I reached down again and took a handful. I am very fond of fresh-picked lychees.

"Where did you get these delicious lychees, Tehura?" I asked.

"Come, I show you," she replied, taking my hand. We left the house, crossed the lanai, and descended the steps. As we passed the spirit stone, Tehura paused and bowed, holding her hands palms outward toward the stone in a gesture of reverence. Then she walked on, gaily picking a hibiscus blossom from a bush and placing it in her hair.

She took me inland on a trail through the ancient forest that ascends the slopes of the mountain to the east. This woodland is filled with *keawe* and *opiuma* trees, coconut palms and monkey-pods. Many of the tree trunks are blanketed with the huge leaves of monstera vines, and *taro* grows in the low places. There are *ti* plants everywhere, and as I paused to smell the spike of some flowering white ginger, I saw the buttress-rooted trunk of a towering cotton tree, its branches high above loaded with green pods.

I looked around me with wonder. Here I was in the dream world walking through an enchanted forest with an equally enchanting woman, an exotic Tahitian who seemed to have come to life out of a painting I had seen as a boy. I was suddenly aware that I could still hear Michael and Christina drumming. I looked at the woman walking with me and wondered if she could hear it, too.

I never found out because Tehura suddenly pointed with delight. There ahead of us was a dark green lychee tree loaded with clusters of the dusky, rose-colored fruit. She picked some and gave them to me. My mind filled with questions as I sat down on a broad stone below the tree.

"Tehura . . . where did you come from, and how did you get here?"

Her eyes regarded me levelly for long moments, then she said, "I came from my island far to the south. I was summoned. I came on a canoe. The crew dropped me on the beach below the *marae*. Then they left." She stopped speaking as though her answer was complete. I was aware that she had used the Tahitian word *marae* instead of the Hawaiian word *heiau*, reinforcing her statement of her place of origin.

"Tehura," I persisted. "Who summoned you? And have we ever met before?" Once again, she regarded me with gravity. Then she spoke, her words a mixture of French and English.

"I was born long ago and lived my life on the island of Tahiti, far to the south across the ocean. I had a good life filled with friends and family, joys and sorrows. At the end of my life, I went into a dream and didn't wake up." Her eyes squinted with effort, as though she were trying to express something she understood well but for which she lacked concepts in English. "I have been in the dream ever since," she continued. "I live in the dreaming of my island, for islands dream, too, you know, just as we humans do."

Then Tehura looked at me strangely and said something totally unexpected. "Sometimes in my dreaming, I can see into a room. It is as though I can look through a window into this very big room with many paintings on the walls. There is nothing else in this room, only paintings. Sometimes the room is empty, but often, I can see many people walking around in the room. They come and look through the window at me, as though they can see me, but when I try to talk with them, they never answer. I found this frightening at first, but I have gotten used to it. It is a very strange dream."

For long moments, I was simply speechless at the implications of what she had just revealed. "Tehura," I finally said, "did you ever meet a painter on your island, a Frenchman who came from Paris?"

"Ah, but of course . . . it was Monsieur Paul. He used to make paintings of me and my friends. He was my lover until he went away and didn't return." Her eyes turned sad. "He was a very unhappy man. That one had many sorrows inside him. I tried to make him happy. . . ." Her words drifted off as her eyes filled with tears.

For long moments, her eyes flowed freely, the tears coursing down her brown face. My thoughts were filled with questions, but this didn't seem an appropriate moment. Instead, I got up from the stone and took her hand, drawing her back down the trail toward the beach. We walked in silence until we could see the pond through the trees. To one side rose the stone wall of the *heiau*. Tehura dried her tears then and turned to me.

"I was summoned to come to this place in my dreaming. I did not know who was calling me or why, but the request was so strong, so I came. Now that I am here, I know who called me, but I still don't know why."

"Who called you, Tehura?"

Her eyes turned to regard the massive shape of Mauna Loa rising like a dark wall to the east. "There is a powerful spirit that lives in this mountain. Like me, she came from the south long ago. It was she who called me."

Pele! Of course . . . she was the spirit of this place. I thought about my meeting with her only days before and understood. But how had she known of my boyhood attraction for the girl in the painting? It was at this moment that I heard the rhythm of the drumming change, calling me back.

"Tehura, would you like to be the caretaker of my garden? Would you like to live here in my house and care for it in my absence?" Her eyes began to sparkle as I said this, and she smiled broadly in response. I took this as a yes. The drum was beckoning, and I had no time to continue.

"You are welcome here. Please stay. I will return soon," I promised, "but for now, I must go." I turned to climb the steps of the *heiau,* then paused and plucked one more scarlet hibiscus blossom. I ascended quickly to the top, then walked across the platform and placed the flower on the altar, an offering to the spirit who lives in the mountain. Then I closed my eyes as the drumming ceased, and my primary focus shifted back to the workshop room.

I thought about this journey a great deal as the week came to a close. I was very much aware that a Western-trained psychiatrist might categorize what I had experienced as a fantasy or daydream, and conclude that I was just simply making the whole thing up with my creative imagination. When I created the thought-form of my house, I was indeed using my creative imagination in combination with my focused intentionality, but what of Tehura? What about the things she said that I *hadn't* created?

Once again, the cognitive investigator might be inclined to say that in these instances, it was my subconscious at work, filling in details, making the whole illusion more interesting, and here is where I beg to differ.

Through my investigations of the inner worlds over the past 15 years, I have come to understand that the creative imagination is a function of the conscious mind/ego. The subconscious *ku* is not creative, but like the inner hard drive of a computer, one of its primary functions is memory. In this sense, it is incapable of making anything up—it can only inform the egoic inner director of what it already knows. But it can observe and send what it perceives to the conscious ego.

In my shamanic journeywork, I often begin the session by instructing my *ku* to bring up the memory of a place I have experienced in either ordinary or nonordinary reality. Then I become the bridge between my here and my there. I simply instruct my *ku* to open the inner doorway, and I then go through it to that place. My *ku* is the aspect of myself through which the journey is both experienced and perceived, yet while I am in these subjective, dream environments, my inner director can still make decisions.

This means that I can determine the course of the action to a certain extent, but there comes a point when things begin to happen that I am not creating with my intentionality, and it is then that I understand quite clearly that I have shifted into a level of reality and experience that has its own existence separate from myself. This is what it means to *vision*.

Like Hakai in Nainoa's time and place, I have discovered through repeated visits to my secret garden that all the elements that make it up, both animate and inanimate, are conscious and alive to some degree, and all can be communicated with for greater understanding. I have learned through direct experience that when I change my garden, my life changes in response. This is a place of extraordinary power and beauty in which I now do much of my spiritual work, and so I frequently invite my spirit helpers, as well as my spirit teacher, to meet with me there in order to accomplish various things. When I do healing work for others, for example, I sometimes invite their spiritual essence to come into my garden where my spirit helpers and I can work on them.

Tehura continues to live in my garden as its *kahu*, or honored caretaker. I would like to add that she is not some dream lover or manifested fantasy from childhood. I have come to accept that she is the soul-spirit of a wise Polynesian woman who lived over a hundred years ago and who has become a close and trusted friend. Often when I am overly stressed or my physical body is in pain from held tension, I go to my garden, and Tehura works on me, relieving the pain by releasing the tension with her strong hands.

I have come to suspect that all of us have such a personal place of power in the inner worlds of dream, and in sharing this information with you, the reader, I encourage each of you to find it.

(From *Visionseeker,* Hay House, 2001)

Stuart Wilde

Author and lecturer **Stuart Wilde** is an urban mystic, a modern visionary; he has written 17 books on consciousness and awareness, including the very successful Taos Quintet, which are considered classics in their genre. They are: *Miracles, Affirmations, The Force, The Quickening,* and *The Trick to Money Is Having Some!*

Stuart's perceptive and quirky way of writing has won him a loyal readership over the years. He has a simple way of explaining things that hitherto have seemed a mystery. His books have been translated into 15 languages.

Websites: **www.stuartwilde.com** and **www.redeemersclub.com**

HERE A PENNY,
THERE A PENNY . . .

I believe that it's important to accept all the money that comes your way. That means that you can't see a penny on the sidewalk and walk past it. You'll have to be consistent in your affirmation, and pick up each and every penny you find—even the horrible ones that are stuck to the pavement with chewing gum. The reason for this is that the collective unconscious, or Universal Law, as I like to call it, isn't aware of value. If you affirm, "I am abundant; money comes to me," and then see a penny in the street and can't be bothered to pick it up, the message you put out by your action is not in sync with your affirmation; thus, you disempower your abundance consciousness.

Now, sometimes picking up a penny, especially when you're with other people, can be embarrassing, for they don't do things like that. They're much too important to accept something for nothing. But the fact that it's embarrassing is excellent training, for you have to go past that idea and act for yourself, not in accordance with what others might think.

Some years ago in London, I was entertaining a group of very important business folk from the U.S. I'd decided to take them to the ballet at the Royal Opera House, Covent Garden. I thought that this would be a nice, swanky way of showing them the top of the line. Now in those days, I'd been banned from driving for having too much blood in my alcohol stream, so I'd bought a Rolls and hired a chauffeur to get around the transport problem.

I had arranged for the driver, Slick Vic, I called him, to wait at the curb directly outside the Opera House so that at the end of the performance I could whisk my guests off to a late-night dinner. A table for five had been reserved at the Trattoria Cost-a-Lotto.

Well, as we came out of the Opera House, crowds milling about, guests in tow, I began to cross the sidewalk to the car. There to my left was a penny. It had been raining that evening, so the penny shone, reflecting the streetlights and the shadows of those lights, flickering as they did through the crowd, giving the momentary impression that the coin was, in fact, winking, taunting me to walk past it. I hesitated, wondering what everyone would think as I groped around at their feet. Then I decided that an affirmation is an affirmation, so I went for the penny.

The problem was that I was a little halfhearted, and instead of just bending down and picking the damn thing up, I did a kind of bunny dip, which entails keeping your back straight, bending your knees, and dropping your hand slightly behind you. The maneuver was taught to waitresses at the Playboy Club as a way of setting drinks on a table without having customers look down their cleavage. I can't remember who taught it to me—deep in the back of my mind there's a faint, fond memory—but something must have been lost in the passage of time, for on that night, I got it all wrong.

What should have been a graceful scoop turned into a fiasco. I hit the penny with my knuckles, and it began a long, loping run across the sidewalk, snaking gracefully in and around many an expensive shoe. At that point, I should have left well enough alone. But determined as I was, I refused to give up. I lunged at the itinerant coin and missed, winding up on all fours.

That night I'd chosen to wear a white satin suit, God knows why. But by the time I finally had the penny in hand, I had acquired most of the muddy water on that particular sidewalk. Meanwhile, Slick Vic had ushered my guests into the car, and they relaxed to watch my pantomime with restrained astonishment.

I was really embarrassed. And once in the car, I felt I had to offer an explanation. So I told my American friends that the penny routine was an ancient British custom that brought untold amounts of good fortune. They were fascinated to learn the ins and outs of the British culture, and one of them even began taking a few notes.

All was well until one of the blokes started to pin me down as to exactly how the "penny in the gutter" routine entered British folklore. At that point, I went completely over the top. I told them that it was a custom handed down from Elizabethan times. To make it real, I created a whole fantastic scenario with Elizabeth and Lord Dudley. I even slung in Walter Raleigh out of politeness, thinking that perhaps my guests were none too familiar with Dudley's exploits. It wasn't long before I had Queen Elizabeth, Lord Dudley, and Walter Raleigh crawling across the floor of Hampton Court in chase of the Royal Penny.

Everyone was duly impressed with my knowledge of the more obscure parts of English history, as was I. I somehow felt that I had created a historic moment returning the "penny in the gutter" to its rightful place among the glories of the English-speaking people. You can just see it:

1558: Elizabeth ascends to the throne of England.
1559: The "Penny in the Gutter" enters English history.

Notes taken, events chronicled, the conversation drifted to silence. As the Rolls glided silently through the night, taking us to our rendezvous with fettuccine, linguine, and Chianti Classico, I thought about the events of the evening. I must say that secretly, I felt proud of myself, damn proud. From time to time, I surreptitiously opened my hand to glimpse the great but muddy prize, while I mused that there's no limit to abundance when you're committed to going for it.

(From *The Trick to Money Is Having Some!,* Hay House, 1989, 1998)

Carnie Wilson

Martin Mann

Born the daughter of Marilyn Wilson and Beach Boy legend Brian Wilson, **Carnie Wilson**, the author of the books *Gut Feelings;* its sequel, *I'm Still Hungry;* and the cookbook *To Serve with Love,* has overcome a lifelong struggle with obesity to achieve personal satisfaction, professional success, and new dimensions of physical and emotional health.

As a young child growing up in the fast lane, Carnie turned to food for comfort. As she grew into adulthood and achieved success with the multiplatinum pop group Wilson Phillips, her dysfunctional relationship with food led to life-threatening morbid obesity. In the summer of 1999, she made the dramatic decision to undergo state-of-the-art weight-loss surgery live over the Internet. Over the next two years, her life was transformed as she lost more than 150 pounds, married the man of her dreams, and fashioned a new future of exciting career opportunities.

Carnie and her husband, Rob, are living in Los Angeles with their daughter, Lola, and their three dogs.

IT WAS ABOUT
LOVE . . .

O n my 31st birthday—April 29, 1999—fate gave me a terrifying present.

I was in Medford, Oregon, doing a concert with Al Jardine. We were getting toward the end of the set where we'd do this nonstop medley of the upbeat Beach Boys songs—"Surfin' Safari," "Fun, Fun, Fun," "Surfin' USA"—those great feel-good songs that just call for dancing.

I had been touring with Al only intermittently over the last 18 months, so I wasn't really used to performing. But as usual, I started jumping around on the stage because it's impossible not to move when you're singing those songs.

I wanted to put on an especially good show that night, because Tiffany Miller, one of my longtime best friends, had come to see me perform. The band and the crowd had sung "Happy Birthday" to me, they'd brought a cake onstage, and I was feeling so happy I had to dance.

I've always been self-conscious about my dancing—worried about my stomach jiggling, my double chin shaking, and all my body fat rippling everywhere. The thought of it embarrassed me, and I didn't want anyone to see.

But once I got up on the stage, something would always happen. The music would shoot through me. I would feel this rush inside my body and start dancing, and suddenly I wouldn't care.

By the end of the show, I'd be drenched with sweat and out of breath. I would ask my sister, Wendy, "Are you out of breath? Are you tired?" Because I wondered whether it was legitimate that I should be tired. Or was it just because of my weight?

Wendy would say, "I'm exhausted." And I would look, and she'd be sweating, too. I'd think, *Oh, thank God I'm not the only one.*

So on that night, I was thinking, *It's my birthday, and my friends are watching. I'm going to give this my all.* Even though I was 298 pounds—heavier than I'd ever been in my whole life—I was going to jump around if it killed me.

So I danced extra hard, and the stage began to bounce. *I'm going to break the stage,* I thought. *Aw, screw it. I'll just dance a little lighter.* But dammit, I wanted to dance hard. So I did.

After the show, it really, really hit me. Something was different this time. I didn't feel right.

I was talking to my friends, and everyone was very excited. But I felt unusually tired, hot, and sweaty, and I couldn't catch my breath.

Tiffany asked, "Are you okay?"

My heart was racing, and my pulse was pounding in my head. There was pain in my right arm, and I could feel my blood getting thicker and hotter in my body, especially around my ears and neck and chest.

"I have to sit down right now," I told her. She looked at me, and I could tell that she was scared.

"I'll be all right," I said. "I just need to rest for a minute."

I told myself to stop and bring my blood pressure down by being calm, taking deep breaths, and drinking a glass of water. I was afraid I was going to have a heart attack any moment.

After a while, I began to cool down, my breath came back, and the pounding and pain went away. But I knew this was a warning I couldn't ignore.

⌒

Doing the shows with Al changed my life in more ways than one. It gave me the courage to just get my ass out on that stage, no matter how big I was. And it put me in touch with how far I'd let my health go.

I remember people saying, "You're so much fun to watch. You've got great charisma onstage." But I was very self-conscious about my size, and it was difficult and frightening to do those shows because I was so fat that my heart felt like it was going to explode.

But when I wasn't performing, I was working hard at just being by myself, which I think is so important. And I started to think a lot about what I wanted in a relationship—and what I didn't want.

I had always had similar patterns in my relationships, and those behavioral patterns were jealousy and insecurity. Maybe it was because I didn't get the attention from my dad that I needed as a girl. Not having that genuine affection and connection made it hard for me to believe that any boy or man in my life really loved me. I didn't feel worthy or deserving of that kind of love because I couldn't recognize it. I didn't know what it was, and I didn't know what to do with it.

It was difficult for me to let someone love me. I'd spent five and a half years with Steven, my ex-boyfriend, and he was a very sweet person with a great heart. For some of that time I thought I was in love, but I think we both deceived ourselves for a long while. He had some of his own pain that I felt responsible for, and I tried to solve everything, but I couldn't. I felt like I let go of myself because I was always worrying about him or us, and why things weren't right.

I was relieved when we both agreed it would be better if we separated and that we shouldn't get married. Finally, we realized that we'd be happier apart because we were so unhappy together. We fought all the time, and I smoked my brains out to keep from getting real with myself about our relationship. I can't speak for Steven, but it wasn't what I wanted it to be, and it didn't feel good anymore. I had known for a long time that it needed to end, but I was too scared to be alone.

I'd lost all my money. I had no job. I was 275 when we broke up, and then I put on another 15 pounds in the months after that. I felt like shit.

I said to myself, "Maybe the relationship with Steven didn't work out because I wasn't happy with myself." But looking back on it now, I'm just so grateful for that experience with him, because it made me go deep into myself about my own problems with intimacy and trust, and it prepared me for something authentic.

I'm so grateful to Al, too, because if it weren't for him, I wouldn't have met Rob.

We were doing a show at the naval base in Willow Grove, Pennsylvania. It was a show for military veterans called VetRock. They had Steppenwolf, War, the Rascals, the Animals—all these '60s bands. Wendy and I were actually the only girls on the whole bill.

I was wearing these huge muumuus when I performed, and I was feeling really big.

It was like, here's Wendy, looking so hot in her beautiful dresses and her beautiful figure, and then here's me—good singer, good charisma onstage, but just a fat blob. I was just feeling really yucky.

But the funny thing is that the day I met Rob, I remember feeling really pretty. I was wearing these little butterfly clips in my hair, and I was happy with my makeup. I said to myself, "You're a big girl, but you're going to put on this outfit, you're going to do the best you can, and you're going to go out there and be proud of who you are."

I was backstage, feeling a little nervous as usual. The crowd was huge, and America—one of my favorite bands in the world—had just finished a really cool set. It was a while before we were due to go on, and I was hungry. So I said to everyone, "Let's go get something to eat."

We went to this huge food tent, and as I was on my way to the buffet line, I saw these two guys walking over on the other side of the tent. I especially noticed the one with the dark hair, and I thought, *Ooh, that is a really cute guy.* Then I turned my attention to the food.

So while I was standing in line, this guy with big frizzy hair came up to me.

"Hey, hi, Carnie. My name is Ken Sharp," he said. "I want to thank you because I wrote you a letter on the Internet and you responded to me, which was cool. I really want to thank you for it." He told me he was a freelance writer, and that he'd be interviewing Al after the show.

"I think we're all going to go to dinner," he said.

I said, "Oh, great."

Then he said, "I'd like you to meet my friend, Rob Bonfiglio."

It was the really cute guy from across the tent. He had this big smile on his face, and I thought, *My God, this guy has the most gorgeous teeth I've ever seen in my life. What a great smile.*

He shook my hand and said, "Hi, Carnie, it's really great to meet you. I saw your talk show, and I want you to know that I really enjoyed watching you." I got a little tingle in my belly. I thought, *That was a really sweet thing to say. What a sweetheart.*

"Thank you," I said, and I felt really shy and didn't know what else to say, because that's the way I really am. I can be totally bold and brazen when I want to, but underneath I'm this totally shy girl—a *perverted* shy girl, if that makes any sense.

Rob asked, "Hey, would you mind if I had my picture taken with you?"

And I thought, *Oh, how cute.*

"Of course," I said. "Of course I wouldn't mind."

So Ken took a picture, and Rob put his arm around me, and his arm was shaking. *Oh my God,* I thought. *He's so nervous. What a munchkin.*

And that was it.

They said, "Have a great show. We'll be out in the front, and we'll see you later." And they walked off.

I thought, *How sweet,* and we ate our lunch.

When I went onstage, I saw all these people in the front row, and there was Rob. I couldn't keep my eyes off him.

And he was staring at me.

I was thinking, *Wait a minute. Is he staring at me?* Because I was so used to all the guys checking Wendy out. I was so excited that it made my day. Rob stood there with the biggest smile on his face I've ever seen, this enormous grin from ear to ear. He was mouthing the words, and when I sang "Darlin'," he just lit up like the most precious thing.

He is such a sweetheart, I thought.

So I sang the whole concert to him because I was just thrilled. I didn't know anything about him. I thought he was Ken's assistant. I had no idea he was a musician.

So we finished the show, and when we went backstage, Rob was there. I was out of breath, and I felt like this sweaty pig.

"That was a great show," Rob and Ken said. "That was so much fun. You did a great job." And they wanted to give me a hug.

Oh my God, I thought, *I'm sweating really bad. I hope I don't smell bad.*

Later on, Rob told me that one of the first things he noticed about me was how good I smelled and how much he loved the smell of my perfume. It's called "Happy" by Clinique, and I still wear it every day because I know he loves it—and I love it, too. It makes me happy because it reminds me of when we first met.

After the show, I'd forgotten that Ken was interviewing Al and we were all going to be together at dinnertime. We went back to the hotel, and there was Rob waiting in the lobby. My heart skipped a beat when I saw him, and I got really nervous. I started to notice that there was something almost magnetic going on with us. I was really attracted to him physically, and I was feeling like he was this adorable shy guy, totally the type I'm attracted to.

I changed, put my hair in a ponytail, and felt really cute as we walked to dinner, but I was too shy to walk beside him. When we sat down to dinner, I didn't have the nerve to sit next to Rob. Al, Ken, Rob, and Wendy sat at one table, and I sat at a separate table with Ritchie Canata and Adam Jardine, staring at Rob's back. The entire dinner I kept telling them, "I've got a crush on that guy right there."

The evening sunlight was coming through the window, and Rob was wearing glasses and a magenta sweater. He was so gorgeous with those beautiful eyes and the sunlight on his face. I was getting horny and thinking, *This guy is so hot. I wonder if he'd be interested in me?* It was just fabulous.

But I didn't know what to do. I didn't know how to approach it. So after dinner, we walked back to the hotel, and I remember just saying, "Nice to meet you guys. Bye-bye." And it was over.

I went home, and I didn't really think twice about it. In my heart, I didn't have the self-confidence to believe that there was any way he'd come after me, and I'd never really dated before. Someone had always set me up or I went out with someone I already knew.

I had no idea how to go about it, or if anything would come of it. But I knew I liked him.

About a week later, I was on the Internet checking out the Wilson Phillips message board, and I saw a letter to Carnie from Rob Bonfiglio. *Rob Bonfiglio?* I thought, *Who? Who the hell is that? I don't know a Rob Bonfiglio.*

Then I read the letter, and it said, "I'm Ken's friend. I met you backstage, and you were so gracious and kind. I really enjoyed meeting you and watching you onstage. It was a great show, really fun, and by the way, I think you're really beautiful."

My heart just melted. I mean, flatter me and forget it. I'm yours. That's just it—especially from a cute guy.

I thought to myself, *You know what? I'm going to have some balls here, some chutzpah. I'm going to write this guy back, and I'm going to ask him if he's single. Why the hell not?*

He had asked in his e-mail about my interests, so I wrote him a nice long letter, and I said, "P.S. Are you single?"

He wrote back and told me all about himself. He was a musician and a writer in a group called Wanderlust that had just made a record. He loved jazz and had graduated from Berklee College of Music in Boston.

I was getting really turned on. *Wow, this guy has made records, he's been on tour, he even opened up for The Who. This guy's so cool. He's like this rock guitar player!* I wondered if we were going to start any kind of dating, or if we were going to see each other, because he lived in Philadelphia.

At the end of his letter, he wrote: "Yes, I'm single."

I wrote back: "Here's my phone number if you ever want to call me."

And he called me that day.

We started talking over the phone, getting to know each other. I loved his voice and how gentle, delicate, and very sweet he was. It was the beginning stage of a relationship where you're really nervous talking to each other, but it's really fun to get to know that person.

And I loved it because he knew what I looked like. He knew my whole deal, and he was still interested. He was really excited to get to know me over the phone, and then we realized that we'd been talking every day for two hours. I was getting excited because I thought, *I think we're going to start dating.*

We had spent about a month on the phone, when we decided it was time to see each other again, even though we lived on opposite sides of the country. I flew him up to Portland, Maine, in July for our show there, and I got him a hotel room because I figured we were really getting close on the phone, but there was no way that we were going to sleep together. I still had *some* values!

He'd been telling me how excited he was about giving me a kiss—and I was just as excited about being kissed and kissing him. So when he got off the plane, it was the cutest thing I've ever seen. He gave me this quick little peck.

I was so excited just to walk around with him. We went for our first meal together at this little place where they served Armenian wraps. I remember walking down the street thinking, *My feet are going to kill me by the time we get to this restaurant*—and it was only a block away. I had only one pair of shoes that were comfortable for me to wear at this point because I was walking on the sides of my feet. I was so heavy I couldn't keep my ankles from rolling over.

Rob was walking at a normal pace—maybe a little fast—and I was really struggling to keep up with him. I was so ashamed and embarrassed, but I didn't want Rob to know.

This was only the second time I'd been with him, and I didn't want him to see me like this. *He's going to be turned off,* I thought.

We got to the little restaurant and ordered our food. I remember being so careful to take small bites. I wanted him to think that I wasn't as hungry as I really was; that I always ate slowly and gracefully; and that I was delicate, feminine, and attractive.

When I was really fat, I thought that if somebody saw me eating, they'd feel that I was a glutton who didn't deserve that food. "Why should *you* be eating? Why should *you* put food into your mouth? Look at your body!"

That's how I was feeling. I was very embarrassed eating in front of him, but it was our first meal together, and I could see that food was very important to Rob. He loves to eat, and I do, too. I still do. So it was a very special thing, and I didn't want to do anything to spoil it.

Rob recently asked me if I remembered our first meal and how special it was.

I told him I did, but in the back of my mind, I was also thinking about what an intense emotional experience it was for me. So I have such compassion for overweight men and women who feel self-conscious about putting food in their mouths in public. I understand why there are so many closet eaters—because people are just so damn ashamed.

I did the concert, and we were together every moment we could manage. After the show, the airline sponsoring the tour put on this beautiful lobster dinner. As we were eating, I said to him, "I want you to kiss me right now."

"But everyone's watching," he said.

"I don't care," I said. "Kiss me right now."

So he gave me this soft, open-mouthed kiss—not like Frenching—but nice, gentle, and very sensual. I felt like a different person from the fat blob who could hardly walk that afternoon.

It was the first time I'd ever had clams, and of course, I was making jokes.

"I hear these are aphrodisiacs," I said, "so let's just keep shoving 'em in." We were thrilled because we knew that after dinner we were going back to the hotel together. I didn't know if he was going to sleep in his room and I was going to sleep in mine, but we both knew we were going to make out for the first time.

We went back to the hotel flushed with that great feeling you have after a wonderful meal.

I went to my room, took a nice bath, lit candles, put on my pretty perfume, and Rob walked in wearing tortoise-shell glasses. I thought it was the cutest, most sophisticated thing ever. He was so cute, so strikingly good-looking. We were totally nervous, but it was the most romantic couple of hours ever. He spent an hour and a half touching and kissing my face. It was like nothing I've ever done, so sensitive and delicate and sweet. The rest of the details are private, but we didn't go all the way. It was just so special that I was a goner from that moment on.

We continued seeing and talking to each other as much as we could, but Rob was in Philadelphia and I was in Los Angeles, so most of our moments together were over the phone. A couple of months after we met, I mentioned to Rob that I was thinking about having weight-loss surgery.

He told me I was beautiful just the way I was, but if my weight bothered me, then it bothered him.

"This surgery is really drastic," I said, "and it's a permanent thing. It would be changing the way my organs are inside. What do you think of that?"

"Is it safe?" was the first thing he wanted to know.

"Yes," I said.

"Then I think it's a great idea," he said. "If you're going to help yourself and it's going to make you feel better, then I totally support it."

"That's great," I said, "because I'm really going to need your support for this. I'm really scared, and this is extreme."

He said to go for it, and when I heard him say that, it definitely validated something for me, because I had this feeling I was going to be with him for a long time—and I wanted to make sure I'd be around to love him and be loved by him.

In the middle of the summer, I spent ten days with Rob in Philadelphia. He was really eager to show me his hometown, and it was great to meet his family. I had a wonderful time, but I was very embarrassed and sad because I was so heavy. I had only two pairs of shoes I could wear that didn't hurt my feet. It wasn't really the shoes, but my feet, that were killing me.

Rob took me to a quaint place called Peddler's Village, with cobblestone streets and little hills and a big outdoor shopping mall. I was huffing and puffing, trying to keep up with him, trying to slow him down, turning my head to exhale so he wouldn't see me gasping for air. I was miserable.

Here I was with my new boyfriend, wanting desperately to be fun and to enjoy myself with him, just trying to do something so normal, and struggling with it every minute. In my heart, I was ashamed of myself and so frustrated and afraid he'd be disappointed and disgusted.

"I'm really embarrassed," I said. "I'm sweating like a pig."

"So what?" he said. "So am I." He was so kind and thoughtful, and he knew I was having a very hard time, but he didn't want me to worry.

"How are you doing?" he'd ask. "Are you all right?"

I'd say, "Yeah." But we both knew it was really difficult for me. And all I could think about was, *I've got to have this operation. I've going to start taking care of myself. I'm doing it. I'm finally going to do something about it.*

I was in love, and I had to protect that love. I couldn't let anything stop me.

I never really imagined that I would fall in love like that. I'd had loves before, and I'd never want to hurt anyone by saying that they weren't the real thing. But I'd never felt this kind of beautiful connection with anyone in any relationship in my life. Rob was my true love, the man my heart had always longed for, and I couldn't risk losing him and the life we could share together.

I knew that it was more than just about my health or my career.

Now it was about love. . . .

(From *Gut Feelings*, Hay House, 2001)

Eve A. Wood, M.D.

Sabra Studiois

Eve A. Wood, M.D., is Clinical Associate Professor of Medicine at the University of Arizona Program in Integrative Medicine. She's the award-winning author of the books *There's Always Help; There's Always Hope* and *10 Steps to Take Charge of Your Emotional Life.* She has written numerous articles for medical and professional publications, is a frequent speaker at national workshops and conferences, and is a pioneer in the field of integrative psychiatry.

Uniting body, mind, and spirit In One™ —in an empowering treatment model—Eve helps people take charge of their emotional lives. She lives in Tucson with her husband and four children.

Website: **www.DrEveWood.com**

The Rebirth
of a Dream

I want to share a personal tale that demonstrates how openness to the creative healing force can transform a painful experience into one of joy. The story began a long time ago, in my home in Philadelphia; and in a kingdom far, far away.

As far back as I can remember, I dreamed of marriage and children. Growing up, I visualized my adult-self sharing a life with a loving husband and four children whom I would call my own. I saw myself raising two girls and two boys. Don't ask me why that was. I can't possibly tell you. I really do not have the faintest idea. Why we dream what we dream is a spiritual question that cannot be fully answered; it's like trying to reduce the infinite to the realm of cognition. It's one of the questions we will ask but may never answer during our time on this planet.

What I can tell you, however, is that my life didn't quite unfold according to my childhood vision. Although I did find and marry a loving man early enough to build the life I dreamed of, the demands of medical school and my psychiatric residency training didn't support it. I chose to put off conceiving my first child until I'd been married for more than six years. As a result, I had only two sons by the time I was in my mid-30s, but no daughters; and for reasons that are irrelevant to this story, I wasn't in a position to attempt further pregnancies. My pain was like a bottomless pit.

Years passed, and each time the notion of daughters crossed my mind, my spirit would weep. The passage of time didn't seem to heal my wound. The pain just wouldn't go away. Then one day I was sitting with my patient, Rachel, who longed for children but couldn't conceive. I found myself responding to the pain of her predicament by saying, "There are other ways to become a parent, Rachel. Have you ever considered adopting a child? You don't need to live with this pain forever."

Rachel looked at me in awe. A smile as bright as the sun itself appeared on her countenance. "You're brilliant," she said. "How did you know to say that?"

Stunned at her remarkable response, I answered, "I don't really know, Rachel. It just came to me, and I said it. I'm touched by how much my words affected you. Trust your reaction to them, and do what your inner wisdom is telling you to do about your life. This is all for a reason."

Rachel did go on to adopt an adorable child from Russia. She transformed her life through that one moment in my office.

What's even more amazing to me about what I'd said is the role they came to play in my own life. For on the day of that session with Rachel, those words had a powerful resonance for me as well. They continued to echo in my brain as I drove home from work. Suddenly, as if the Messiah had stepped into my car, I found myself saying aloud, "I can do that! I can adopt a child. In fact, I can do that more than once. I can have four children! I can have two daughters. I can give wonderful lives to two children who might otherwise not have that opportunity. I will live my dream after all!"

As I entered the door of my home, my spirit was singing. My husband looked up at me from his place at the table and said, "You have that look in your eyes. I know that look! What's going on?"

I gazed back at him, unable to put this wonderful idea into words. He began to guess.

"Are we taking a vacation?"

I shook my head.

"Are we moving?" Again I shook my head.

"Bigger than that," I said. "I want to adopt a child." My husband's face betrayed his awe and fear. "In fact," I continued, "I want to do it twice. I want to adopt two little girls who need families. I want to have those two daughters I always dreamed of having. My spirit is singing, and I must dance."

After hours of conversation, my husband took a deep breath and looked at me. "I know how you are when the fire starts burning. There's no stopping you. You've seen the future and you'll rush to grasp it. . . . So, what do you need me to do?"

The well of pain that I'd harbored for so long suddenly turned to overflowing joy. I would have two daughters after all. I would! I would! I would!

Although the journey has been fraught with roadblocks and dead ends, today I'm the mother of four children. I have two sons and two daughters. My sons, Benjamin and Gabriel, are my biological children. And my daughters, Shira and Glory, came to me on the wings of angels. My daughter, Shira Leora, whose name means "song of light," was born in China and became my child when she was ten months old. My other daughter, Glory Beth, was born in Cambodia and became my child when she was three and a half years old.

When Shira first learned that she would be getting a sister, she began to dance around the room. "I'm so excited! I'm so excited! I can't wait! I'm going to have a sister! I'm going to have a sister! I really am!"

When my husband and I took Shira and her grandfather to Cambodia with us, she gained a sister who looked like her . . . and I realized a dream I thought had died.

(From *There's Always Help; There's Always Hope,* Hay House, 2006)

AFTERWORD

"Now that you've read the empowering stories within these pages, I'd like to share a little more about where the inspiration came for my own writings. The following is a portion of the Foreword I wrote recently for The Game of Life and How to Play It, *by Florence Scovel Shinn, originally published in 1925 and reissued by Hay House under the title* The Game of Life *(with a reinterpretation of the text) in 2005."*

— Louise

PLAYING THIS GAME OF LIFE

My own start in the New Thought/self-help field was influenced by several teachers, but the person who impacted me most was Florence Scovel Shinn. She was born in 1871 in Camden, New Jersey. An artist by nature, she married fellow artist Evert Shinn. In 1912, after 14 years of marriage, Evert asked for a divorce. It took some time for Florence to recover from the blow, but when she did, she was through with art and had discovered New Thought philosophy.

In 1925, the year before I was born, she self-published a book called *The Game of Life and How to Play It.* As a metaphysical teacher and lecturer in New York City, Florence became quite popular, holding lectures three times a week. She taught using familiar, practical, and everyday examples. Although she died in 1940, her work still inspires and activates all of us who continue to get value from her books.

In the early 1970s, as I was beginning my own period of study of New Thought ideas, I discovered Florence's books. I felt an immediate connection with her words "Happiness and health must be earned by absolute control of the emotional nature. . . . All the organs are affected by resentment. For when you resent, you resent with every organ of the body. You pay the penalty with rheumatism, arthritis, neuritis, etc., for acid in the thoughts produce acid in the blood. . . . False growths, tumors, etc., are caused by jealousy, hatred, and unforgiveness."

This was a totally new idea to me, and I was electrified by this—so I wished she had gone on for pages so I could learn more, but she only mentioned individual diseases a few more times. However, these ideas sparked something in me, and I had to learn more. My mind just couldn't let the subject drop. I thought, *If this is true for these parts of the body, what are the connecting patterns for diseases in the rest of the body?*

Words and thoughts. Words and thoughts. I began to listen to what people said, how they said it, and the phrases they used. I trained myself over the next few years to listen to the repetitive patterns in people's choice of words and the nature of their complaints. I learned to trust my intuition. I made lists of complaints, and the affirmations I felt would be healing thoughts.

A friend in my study group saw this list and suggested that I make a little booklet and print it. And there the humble beginnings of *Heal Your Body* were sown. Little did I know where this 12-page compilation would take me in time—that it would be the small seed that would lead to the creation of my publishing company, Hay House.

I'm so in awe of where Life has taken me. I've always identified with Florence. She was forceful, simple, dynamic, and to the point, and she put forth powerful affirmations. Florence had an affirmation for everything. I still turn to her when I want to use a strong one.

She's taught me how to play this "Game of Life" very well.

Jill Kramer and Louise L. Hay

ABOUT THE EDITOR

Jill Kramer, originally from the suburbs of Philadelphia, has lived in Southern California since the mid-1980s and has been the editorial director at Hay House for more than 13 happy years. She has a B.S. in TV, Film, and English from Boston University and prior to working for Hay House had a varied career as a photo editor, advertising copywriter, TV and film story analyst, newspaper columnist, and more. She's the author of several books on cats and writes social commentary for various publications.

We hope you enjoyed this Hay House book.
If you'd like to receive a free catalog featuring additional
Hay House books and products, or if you'd like information
about the Hay Foundation, please contact:

Hay House, Inc.
P.O. Box 5100
Carlsbad, CA 92018-5100

(760) 431-7695 or (800) 654-5126
(760) 431-6948 (fax) or (800) 650-5115 (fax)
www.hayhouse.com® • www.hayfoundation.org

Published and distributed in Australia by: Hay House Australia Pty. Ltd.
18/36 Ralph St. • Alexandria NSW 2015 • *Phone:* 612-9669-4299
Fax: 612-9669-4144 • www.hayhouse.com.au

Published and distributed in the United Kingdom by: Hay House UK, Ltd.
292B Kensal Rd., London W10 5BE • *Phone:* 44-20-8962-1230
Fax: 44-20-8962-1239 • www.hayhouse.co.uk

Published and distributed in the Republic of South Africa by:
Hay House SA (Pty), Ltd., P.O. Box 990, Witkoppen 2068
Phone/Fax: 27-11-706-6612 • orders@psdprom.co.za

Published in India by: Hay House Publications (India) Pvt. Ltd.,
Muskaan Complex, Plot No. 3, B-2, Vasant Kunj, New Delhi 110 070
Phone: 91-11-4176-1620 • *Fax:* 91-11-4176-1630 • www.hayhouseindia.co.in

Distributed in Canada by: Raincoast • 9050 Shaughnessy St.,
Vancouver, B.C. V6P 6E5 • *Phone:* (604) 323-7100
Fax: (604) 323-2600 • www.raincoast.com

Tune in to **HayHouseRadio.com**® for the best in inspirational
talk radio featuring top Hay House authors! And, sign up via the
Hay House USA Website to receive the Hay House online newsletter
and stay informed about what's going on with your favorite authors.
You'll receive bimonthly announcements about: Discounts and Offers,
Special Events, Product Highlights, Free Excerpts, Giveaways, and more!
www.hayhouse.com®